"For those who long to be invited and a deeper way of Christian community, Andrew Arndt ushers readers into the light of Jesus' model for both. Make no mistake; this is not a 'sunshine' book—but it is one that explores the deep contours, refractions, and strange but glorious mystery of the whole gospel story."

AUBREY SAMPSON, church planter, teaching pastor, podcaster, and author of several books, including *What We Find in the Dark: Loss, Hope, and God's Presence in Grief* and *The Louder Song: Listening for Hope in the Midst of Lament*

"Jesus' story carries such shimmering beauty and transformative power not only because of what happened two thousand years ago but because of how the story lives now, in the community of God's people. Andrew Arndt, with sentences that sing and simmer, invites us to behold the story anew, to be undone, and to truly live."

WINN COLLIER, author of *Love Big, Be Well* and *A Burning in My Bones* and director of the Eugene Peterson Center for Christian Imagination

"The gospel is good news—not just in theory but in truth, a living reality strong and good enough to permeate our bodies and communities. Pastor Andrew Arndt, like generations of Christians before him, has found a doorway to that living truth in the ebbs and flows of the church calendar. In *A Strange and Gracious Light*, Arndt draws from his years of pastoral wisdom, relational experience, and a pool of scholars as diverse as Kristin Kobes Du Mez and Gustavo Gutiérrez to demonstrate how the good news of Jesus shines transformational light in every season and circumstance of our lives."

CATHERINE MCNIEL, author of *Fearing Bravely: Risking Love for Our Neighbors, Strangers, and Enemies*

"Pastor Andrew is one of the best thinkers and communicators I know. He's a deep well, and this book will stir us to holier and healthier living."

BRADY BOYD, pastor of New Life Church in Colorado Springs

"This is a wonder-filled book. As Andrew Arndt takes us through the church's calendar—from Advent to Pentecost—he beautifully weaves biblical stories with his own powerful testimonies. Together, these stories mysteriously cause to be the world they describe. I urge you to enter this space and experience the ebb and flow of transforming presence."

CHERYL BRIDGES JOHNS, co-director of the Global Pentecostal House of Study at United Theological Seminary

A STRANGE AND
GRACIOUS LIGHT

ANDREW ARNDT

A
STRANGE
AND
GRACIOUS
LIGHT

HOW THE STORY OF JESUS CHANGES
THE WAY WE SEE EVERYTHING

HERALD
PRESS

Harrisonburg, Virginia

Herald Press
PO Box 866, Harrisonburg, Virginia 22803
www.HeraldPress.com

Library of Congress Cataloging-in-Publication Data
Names: Arndt, Andrew, author.
Title: A strange and gracious light : how the story of Jesus changes the
  way we see everything / Andrew Arndt.
Description: Harrisonburg, Virginia : Herald Press, [2025] | Includes
  bibliographical references.
Identifiers: LCCN 2024052874 (print) | LCCN 2024052875 (ebook) | ISBN
  9781513816203 (paperback) | ISBN 9781513816210 (hardcover) | ISBN
  9781513816227 (ebook)
Subjects: LCSH: Jesus Christ--Meditations | Church year meditations. |
  Christian life--Biblical teaching.
Classification: LCC BT306.43 .A76 2025 (print) | LCC BT306.43 (ebook) |
  DDC 242/.3--dc23/eng/20250108
LC record available at https://lccn.loc.gov/2024052874
LC ebook record available at https://lccn.loc.gov/2024052875

Study guides are available for many Herald Press titles at www.HeraldPress.com.

A STRANGE AND GRACIOUS LIGHT
© 2025 by Herald Press
Released by Herald Press, Harrisonburg, Virginia 22803. 800-245-7894. All rights reserved.
Library of Congress Control Number: 2024052874
International Standard Book Number: 978-1-5138-1620-3 (paperback);
      978-1-5138-1621-0 (hardcover); 978-1-5138-1622-7 (ebook)
Printed in United States of America
Cover: iland19 / iStock / Getty Images Plus; zoom-zoom / iStock / Getty Images Plus;
  Prompilove / iStock / Getty Images Plus

29 28 27 26 25   10 9 8 7 6 5 4 3 2 1

To the saints at New Life East:

"They have refreshed my spirit. . . . Recognize such people."
(1 Corinthians 16:18 CSB)

CONTENTS

Foreword 11

Prelude: Why We Gather 13

1 Advent: Waiting for God 29

2 Christmas: Everything Holy.................... 47

3 Epiphany: A Great Light 65

4 Lent: The Weakness of Power, the Power
of Weakness 83

5 Good Friday: Safe with Jesus.................. 101

6 Easter: The Future Does Not Depend on Us........ 119

7 Ascension: To the Heart of Things 135

8 Pentecost: Transfiguring Life 155

Acknowledgments 175

Notes.. 177

The Author.................................. 185

FOREWORD

The first thing I noticed about Andrew Arndt when I met him was the way he listened. We were in a classroom beginning a three-year program that would culminate in a doctor of ministry degree. I was leading a conversation about words and word craft. He was thinking. You could almost see him doing it—connecting dots, finding and forming questions to hold until an appropriate moment. When the appropriate moment came, the questions were the kind that emerge out of substantial reflection—surprising, theologically informed, edgy, and humble. When I had the pleasure of reading his thesis at the end of those three years, I recognized in it the rich fruit of mature, lively, prayerful reflection. He brings to both conversation and writing the heart of a seasoned pastor, the wide reading of a lifelong learner, an astute theological imagination, the sprightliness of a practiced storyteller, and a quality that monk and author Jean Leclercq beautifully called "the love of learning and the desire for God."

I often listen to Andrew's sermons on the New Life East website for the sheer pleasure of hearing exceptional, inspiring preaching. Like those sermons, this book draws on a wide range of literature—Shakespeare, William Blake, Dickinson, Dostoevsky, Yeats, Flannery O'Connor, and Marilynne

Robinson, to name a few. These writers enter these pages as friends and familiars with whom he's been in life-giving conversation. The conversation includes similarly varied theological voices—Calvin, Barth, Von Balthasar, Nouwen, Moltmann, and Gutiérrez, as well as beloved lay theologians like C. S. Lewis and G. K. Chesterton and early ancestors in faith, including the desert fathers, Athanasius, Augustine, Irenaeus, and Julian of Norwich. Andrew somehow manages to draw water from all those deep wells, offering it without pretension but rather with the pleasure of one introducing dear old friends to dear new ones.

The dear new friends he references in every chapter are those he's called to serve every Sunday and most weekdays as preacher, counselor, pastoral caregiver, teacher, and friend. The love Andrew brings to his work is palpable and moving. He not only loves those he prays for; he loves to pray and to dwell in the presence of the one he prays to. This book speaks of prayer in a manner that will enable any reader to imagine what authentic joy can actually be found, even in the thick of electronic overload and constant distraction, in what he might well call, as the old hymn writer did, a "sweet hour of prayer." Andrew awakens many mornings, he says, to Morten Lauridsen's glorious choral work *O magnum mysterium*. And in Andrew I have come to recognize with great gratitude a man who lives, awestruck, at the edge of a great mystery, feet planted firmly in this world, laughter ready, capable of sharing others' sorrows, who knows himself, and us, as God's beloved. This captivating book, a journey through the church year with a skilled and generous guide, is infused with that love.

—Marilyn McEntyre
Author of *Caring for Words in a Culture of Lies* and other books

WHY WE GATHER

I am not ashamed of the gospel, because it is the power of God.

—ROMANS 1:16

The gospel is the story of Jesus, told as a promise.

—ROBERT JENSON, paraphrased from *Story and Promise*

It is June in Colorado, my favorite time of year. Finally, after so many bleak months, it is green and warm here at seven thousand feet above sea level. My alarm goes off early (4:30, to be precise) and I wake up happy and smiling. I have my reasons.

For one, the ringtone on my alarm. I discovered a feature on my phone where I can play a song of my choosing instead of my alarm's usual soul-rattling "beep, beep, beep . . ." I am greeted this morning by Johann Sebastian Bach's Cello Suite No. 1 in G Major, the Prelude, performed by Yo-Yo Ma—a favorite of mine. The warm sounds of the cello wash over my awakening consciousness, reminding me of the world's goodness and beauty. Considering what feels like the crescendoing chaos of our moment in history, this strikes me as a wise way to start a day. Almost an act of defiance. Thank you, Johann and Yo-Yo.

For another, I love being up early. I hail from a long line of early risers on both sides of the family. It's in my blood to be awake before the dawn, about my business. Morning is my time to edge my way mindfully into the day, sniffing around in the darkness for mystery. I am looking, always looking, for God. "Have you seen the one my heart loves?" (Song of Solomon 3:3). That I am at the quest again makes me happy.

But I am smiling for another reason. It is Sunday. And I'm a pastor. I've been at this for the last twenty or so years, and I love my job now more than when I started. I can't believe that I get to do what I do—a childhood dream, fulfilled week after week.

Growing up in church, I can remember watching our pastor open the Scriptures to expound them every Sunday and thinking to myself, from a very early age, "That's what I want to do." And even more: "That's what I was *made* to do."

The feeling has never left me. Mercifully, the Lord has confirmed those early intuitions and desires—opening doors and creating opportunities and calling me into the service of his people as a pastor-preacher. The kindness of it staggers me.

These days I'm pastoring a group of folks on the east side of Colorado Springs, where my wife Mandi and I and our four kids live. We planted this congregation several years ago and love them dearly. They've become family to us. We've been gone for the last ten days on vacation and have missed them fiercely. And so, when Bach's Prelude begins playing and I begin to awaken, so much of my joy is just this: the thought of seeing their faces, gathering with them yet again in worship to sing and pray and preach and come to the Table. A morning spent sharing the bread of love—which is to say, God. It fills my heart with expectation.

Rolling out of bed, I throw on a baseball cap and hoodie and amble downstairs to make the coffee and start working through my morning paces—prayer and devotion and a little theological reading. The usual. I look over my sermon notes one more time and then head out on a pre-church run to clear my head and settle my soul before plunging into the fray.

When I arrive at the school our church calls home, the action begins—and quickly. I connect with my team, walk over to the AV-tech booth to check over my slides, and then head to the front door to greet congregants as they arrive: young and old, single and married, prodigals and I-wouldn't-miss-a-Sunday-for-the-world types, wealthy, middle class, poor; white, Black, brown; immigrant and never-left-the-state'ers. They stream in. The existence of *any* congregation *anywhere* to me is a miracle—a sovereign work of God. And that *this one* exists, *here*, simply staggers me. That somehow, each week, despite everything, the Spirit draws these people out of their homes to share communion with God and one another in an ever-expanding circle of divine love—and this in an increasingly fractured world. The importance of it is never lost on me. The bare fact of our coming together is already and always a sign to me that God reigns.

And we are coming together. Our young church is growing—in fits and starts, no doubt; but slowly and steadily all the same. And by some extravagant mercy, I get a front-row seat. In just a few minutes we'll start in with the singing and hear an announcement or two and greet each other and then I'll stand up, look out on their faces, and say, "Hear the word of the Lord . . ."

WHY DO WE GATHER?

Okay, so maybe you're not a morning person, on any day, let alone—especially—on Sundays. Maybe you've tried church and found it not especially miraculous or merciful. Or maybe it was, but something went terribly wrong. The word of the Lord got twisted, and you got hurt. Or maybe church just doesn't make sense to you. I get it.

If that's you, then this book is for you, too. It seems to me that whatever our reference point to church, we're all holding the same starting question: *Why?* Why do this? What draws us—or at least some of us—to the weekly ritual of corporate worship, to the "communion of saints," as the old creeds put it? What are we looking for? Or to quote Jesus, "What do you *want*?"

Yes. What *do* we want? Such a question.

I have a suspicion.

Some time ago, I spent the better part of a year reading the poetry of a crotchety Welsh priest, R. S. Thomas. A half-century ago he wrote the following poem—a poem that stopped me cold when I read it; a poem that defines for me what we're looking for when we gather:

> A little aside from the main road,
> becalmed in a last-century greyness,
> there is the chapel, ugly, without the appeal
> to the tourist to stop his car
> and visit it. The traffic goes by,
> and the river goes by, and quick shadows
> of clouds, too, and the chapel settles
> a little deeper into the grass.
>
> But here once on an evening like this,
> in the darkness that was about

his hearers, a preacher caught fire
and burned steadily before them
with a strange light, so that they saw
the splendour of the barren mountains
about them and sang their amens
fiercely, narrow but saved
in a way that men are not now.[1]

Thomas, as a rule, was not given to outbursts of euphoria. An atmosphere of cool melancholy lingers about the body of his work like a thick English fog. He is a poet of life's cold cruelties and antagonizing absences.

And yet he also quite clearly believed that our lives, both at the edges and at their depths, are surrounded by the unfathomable, gracious Mystery that is God, by a Presence greater than our absences—a Presence that refuses to be hidden and that here and there shatters the surfaces, dazzling and refreshing with breakthroughs of light that, for all we can tell, seem to come from *somewhere else*. "Strange" light, that is.

Sometimes, Father Thomas thought, such breakthroughs happen in church (imagine that!), where amid humdrum lives, sleepy communities, decaying buildings, gray chapels, sterile school gymnasiums, and lackluster ministries, preachers every now and again catch fire and burn steadily with that strange light—light that illuminates the barren landscapes, revealing their color, awakening fierce affirmation on the lips of God's people.

That, I suggest, is why we gather; *that* is what we are looking for; *that* is what we want—the eruption of fire and light that opens our eyes, that awakens praise, that saves and transforms. We keep coming—in spite of the good reasons many of us have for *not* doing so—because we believe that the eruption of light, and all that the light brings with it, matters.

LIFE IS HAPPENING

Behind the faces that I look out upon on a Sunday morning are stories. I am aware of and involved with many, very many, of them. Here's a sampling:

(Note—I tell a good number of stories in this book. To protect privacy, I've often changed names or substantive details. Where I haven't made such changes, names are used with permission.)

I get down off the platform after giving the benediction and immediately am greeted by a couple in their late forties. Their grown son has been overseas for two years and during that time has decided to undergo a gender transition. They are just finding out about it now and are reeling, understandably. Their son loves both Jesus and his parents and they love him and Jesus too, but they are at a complete loss on how to navigate this altogether new and unexpected terrain.

I take it all in.

"What do you need from me?" I ask.

"Nothing. Just for you to be aware of us. And to pray."

We pray. And I tell them that I will continue to hold them—and their child—in my prayers.

I turn around, and a woman whose husband of fifteen years has decided to leave her is standing in front of me. She didn't see it coming. No, the marriage wasn't perfect—but whose marriage is? She thought they were doing okay. Kids and a mortgage and a circle of friends and a life together. Then one day he wakes up and says he wants out. Just like that. No infidelity. There's not another woman. It's just time for a change. And suddenly their life is in a thousand little pieces—and she's holding all of them.

"I have no idea what the kids and I are going to do," she says. "Why is God letting this happen?" We talk and pray and

I tell her to keep me posted on any developments. I walk away wishing I could wave a magic wand and fix it. A child's wish, but a real one.

I make my way down the hallway to the lobby, where a man known for his passion for politics rushes up to me. A new piece of national legislation has him concerned, and based on what he's read, if local churches do not act decisively to take a stand, so much of what we love will be lost.

"What I'd like to see us do," he says, and then begins to outline his plan for getting our church involved. I hear him out, and then explain that while I appreciate his zeal and agree with him on several points, his plan is not an appropriate use of the church's authority. He is visibly disappointed and requests a meeting to talk about it all in more detail.

I can think of a hundred other ways I'd like to spend an hour on a Wednesday afternoon than talking politics with an impassioned congregant. Trying to write a good sermon, for instance. Or answering emails. Or getting audited. Anything, really.

But I believe that our baptism demands we enter uncomfortable spaces like this with one another, and in truth, the issues he is raising *do* matter, and so much *does* depend on our action, or lack thereof. Beyond that, when I step back to think about it, it astonishes me that in a cultural climate of ecclesial mistrust, someone still actually wants to talk to their pastor about things they care about—politics, even.

So . . . "Sure," I say, "send me an email and we'll get something set up."

In the lobby I run into another couple, a young one. This Sunday is their first back at church in three weeks after losing their baby. The mom was nine months pregnant. Full term. Woke up on her due date—*on her due date*—and didn't feel the baby kicking. Went in to see what was going on. No heartbeat. Had to deliver their little girl stillborn—*a day after* she was supposed to have arrived safe and sound in this warm, wonderful world. Mandi and I sat with them in their living room two days later. They cried the entire time. And we cried too—the warm world suddenly feeling cold, cruel, bleak. "This whole thing is so unthinkable," the young, newly bereaved mom kept saying that day. "Where is God? It all feels so meaningless."

We talked and prayed and I told them I looked forward to seeing them back at church. And now they're here. I hug them. "It's good to see you," I say. "How are you?"

Through tears: "We're here."

That was more than good enough for me.

That is a sliver of a normal Sunday. Surrounding moments such as the ones I've described are dozens of others—beautiful and painful and hilarious and confusing. Life is happening in the congregation. All of it. It's all there. And whatever the surface appearance of a Sunday morning, the stakes are extravagantly high. They could not be higher. We—all of us, for the most part—gather not out of some hackneyed sense of religious obligation, but because life is *just so much*, because it hurts and confuses as much as it delights and dazzles, and we are hungry for meaning in the meaninglessness, for an experience of Mystery in what can feel like bewildering madness.

THE STORIES WE TELL

This is why I think that preaching—and to be more precise, the *subject matter* of our preaching—is so important. The word of God sidles up alongside us in our bewilderment and invites us into a new perception of reality. It challenges the stories we tell—stories we tell about ourselves, others, and the world around us. The challenge will change us, if we'll let it.

An example, straight from the biblical text: 2 Samuel 12. King David is in a hot mess—quite of his own making. Worst part is, he doesn't seem to realize it, or even care. He's violated a married woman, gotten her pregnant, and then leveraged the power of his position to murder her husband and hush it all up.

What is the Lord's response? He sends a prophet, Nathan, *to tell David a story*. "Once upon a time," says Nathan, "there were two men—one rich, and the other poor. The rich man had more than enough cattle. The poor man had only one little lamb. It ate from his hands and drank from his cup and slept in his arms like a child. It was precious to him. One day the rich man had a visitor come to town, and rather than preparing one of his own livestock, he took the poor man's lamb. Slaughtered, butchered, roasted, and devoured it with his visitor, then drained his cup, wiped his mouth, and leaned back in his chair, fat and happy, like he'd done nothing wrong."

David, seething with anger, barely lets Nathan finish. "The man who did this must die!" he blurts out in a rage (A rage, I should add, that borders on incoherence, since David goes on to demand that the rich man "pay back four times over for what he did!" We're inclined to ask: Which outcome, David? Death or payback? Or perhaps you mean payback and *then* death? But whatever. We can see this has stirred you up a bit . . .)

And then, with David's vitriol lingering in the air, Nathan, having masterfully set the trap, now springs it: "You are the man." The story upends David's world, ripping the scales from his eyes, piercing his heart, and the words of Psalm 51 come spilling out. All because of a "once upon a time . . ."

Stories will do that to you. Sometimes they fall upon you like a bolt of lightning or a thunderclap—as with King David. Other times they sneak up on you unawares, stealing past "the watchful dragons of the heart," as C. S. Lewis put it so memorably, dazzling us gradually with the goodness of God.[2]

Another example: John 4—Jesus in conversation at Jacob's well with a Samaritan woman. The story is noteworthy for many reasons, not least for all the objections the woman throws at Jesus—objections that have everything to do with the stories she tells about her sense of self and others, her understanding of her place in the world and her proximity to Presence, to Holiness, *to God*, and the way in which God is accessed.

"You're a Jew; I'm a Samaritan . . ."

"You're a man; I'm a woman . . ."

"You have nothing to draw with and the well is deep . . .
     are you greater than Jacob?"

"You Jews claim we must worship in Jerusalem and not
     here . . ."

"I have no husband . . ."

"When Messiah comes, he will explain everything . . ."

A barrage of objections, each rooted in stories she told herself. And at each stage of the conversation, Jesus lovingly removes them, challenging those stories with a greater, better, truer story—a story that culminates, in Jesus' telling, with the gift of his presence. "I, the one speaking to you—I am he" (John 4:26).

And like David—albeit in a different way, by a different route—the woman is undone. She sprints back to the town to tell her friends and neighbors about a man who told her everything she had ever done, wondering aloud, "Could this be the Messiah?" (4:29). Her buoyant heart and fragmentary knowledge of Jesus spark a revival—the entire town goes out to meet the Lord (4:30).

ONCE UPON A TIME . . .

This is the way the Bible works. "Once upon a time . . ." is the idiom of Scripture, the way it insinuates itself into our lives, our hearts. "In the beginning . . ." says the writer of Genesis (1:1), thus opening a wild tale of weal and woe, of calling and covenant, of catastrophe and calamity, of promise and provision, of agonizing absences and weary nights of weeping, of cross and resurrection and Spirit-sending that culminates finally in the voice of the Almighty shouting from the heavens, "Behold, I make all things new!" (Revelation 21:5 NKJV)— the Bible's version of "and they all lived happily ever after."

The extent to which we believe this story and live by its light is the measure of our transformation. For there are other stories that capture our imaginations. The story of success and achievement, for one. The story of money and power, for another. The story of one nation or people group, one class, culture, or ethnicity over all the others. Too many and too vast to count, these alternative stories. They are all around us. They are the air we breathe.

The problem with them is not just that they are false, but that they do not deliver what they promise. They do not heal. They do not soothe. They do not bring deliverance. In fact, they make everything *worse*, darkening the world with false hopes and empty assurances, fueling our greed and antagonism, plunging us into the endless black night of misery and despair.

We are desperate for a better story. Desperate for the light.

But just what is the "strange light" of which R. S. Thomas spoke that illuminates the barren landscapes? What is it that shatters our taken-for-granted visions of reality and evokes new possibilities for living?

The answer, of course, is the gospel of Jesus Christ, the good news about what God has accomplished for us in the life, death, and resurrection of the man from Nazareth in Galilee. Something about this man and his story turned the world upside-down when it first splashed upon the shores of late antiquity. It still can; it still does. The gospel of Jesus transforms the world.

I feel a tension here—and perhaps you do, too. The tension is with that old word of the church: *gospel*. A cherished word, to be sure; and yet—one not without difficulty. I am tempted to say that the difficulty is with the sheer amount of baggage the word carries—cultural accretions that have little to do with or seriously distort Jesus. (I'm thinking here of so-called "gospel tracts" that look like hundred dollar bills but are actually folded facsimiles that claim to reveal the "plan of salvation" inside; or of sweaty preachers threatening fire and brimstone if the hearers don't repent *and also*, immediately after the altar call, taking up a "love offering" to help with the purchase of a new private jet. You could likely add your own examples.)

Baggage. Lots of baggage.

But perhaps more troubling is that in my conversations with people, more often I find that our sense of "gospel" is not too much but too little; that it has become narrow, limited, constricting, small. It leaves far too much out. For we have been taught to think of the gospel as mere instructions on how to get to heaven, to be presented to our unbelieving neighbors or to the listening congregation at the end of a sermon with an invitation to repent and believe.

I've lived with the gospel for all my life now, and I am sure that it is not *less* than that. But I am likewise convinced that it is something very much *more*—and that that *something more* is intensely powerful. So says Paul, in a justly famous passage in Romans: "I am not ashamed of the gospel, because it is the power of God that brings salvation to everyone who believes: first to the Jew, then to the Gentile. For in the gospel the righteousness of God is revealed" (Romans 1:16–17).

What is the gospel, then? The best definition I know of comes from the late theologian Robert Jenson, who argued that the gospel is, quite simply, *the story of Jesus told as a promise.*[3]

"The story." The *whole* story. Not just a couple bits and pieces of it—death and resurrection, for example—but the whole kit and kaboodle, from the long period of preparation to the incarnation to the miracles and signs *through* the death and resurrection and ascension of the Messiah and the sending of the Spirit at Pentecost, all the way *to* the coming of the new heavens and the new earth. *That* is the gospel. "The story of Jesus, told as a promise."

All my fascination as a preacher—as a *Christian*—lies precisely there. How do we come to grips with all that God has made possible for us in Jesus—with what Paul called the "depth of the riches of the wisdom and knowledge of God" (Romans 11:33), the things no eye had seen and no ear had heard and no imagination had ever conceived but which had now been revealed by the Spirit of God (1 Corinthians 2:9–10)? How do we trust it with our whole lives, learning to walk by its light, strange though it may be—strange, and yet *gracious*; for this light will heal and renew if we'll let it, transforming our lives, *transfiguring* the way we see everything.

That's what this book is about. I've written it as a way to grow into a deeper appreciation of every good thing God has made possible for us in Christ, and how his story is our story, *your* story, and how knowing that changes everything. My hope is that you will come away seeing better how the vision of Christ rendered by New Testament is God's first and last Word over your life, over our lives, over the whole world; how everything, literally everything, belongs in him, finds its ground and meaning in him, and is finally brought to fulfillment in him—in the One who is the Alpha and Omega, the Beginning and the End. As Augustine put it: *Et quis finis, nisi Deus Christus?*—What is the end, but Christ our God?[4]

Jesus is where we're headed.

And that is good news.

Before we get into it, a quick word on method. One of the tried-and-true ways Christians have kept the story of Jesus front and center is the use of the church calendar—the annual sojourn from Advent to Pentecost. Most Christians are familiar, of course, with Christmas and Easter—important moments, no doubt; but only *moments*, movements, chapters within the overall drama of how God has come to rescue us in Jesus. Taken in its entirety, the church calendar puts the *whole* story in front of us, inviting us "to enter by faith" into all God has made possible for us in Christ. Through the church calendar, the story "takes up residence within us and transforms us by the saving and healing presence of Christ," writes theologian Robert Webber. "As we enter the saving events of Jesus, . . . Christ shapes us by the pattern of his own living and dying so that our living and dying in this world is a living and dying in him."[5]

By entering fully into Christ's story, we become as he is.

With that in mind, I've structured this book around the movements of the church calendar, as those movements capture that story best. This isn't an argument for using the calendar, per se (as Saint Augustine is reported to have said, "In essentials, unity; in non-essentials, liberty; in all things, charity") . . . but hey, if it helps you fall more in love with Jesus, why not? Do as you are convicted.

Enough prelude. Let's get started.

Prelude
QUESTIONS FOR DISCUSSION

1. What is it that draws you to church? If you've been away, what keeps you away?

2. "The gospel is the story of Jesus, told as a promise." What do you make of that?

3. Can you think of a time in your life when encountering the story of Jesus has changed you?

1

ADVENT

Waiting for God

I wait for the LORD, my whole being waits,
    and in his word I put my hope.
I wait for the LORD
    more than watchmen wait for the morning,
    more than watchmen wait for the morning.
—PSALM 130:5–6

Above all, trust in the slow work of God.
—PIERRE TEILHARD DE CHARDIN, "Patient Trust"

Years ago, when I was a young pastor serving at a church in the Midwest, a call came in to the church offices. A woman named Laura was in the hospital with a mystery illness. Would we come to pray for her?

I relayed the message to my senior pastor and arranged for us to meet Laura in her hospital room. Laura was a person of great strength and faith, and when we arrived, both were on full display. She described her condition. "Several of my internal organs have gone into sudden failure. The doctors aren't sure why. They're running some tests and we're hoping to have the results soon."

My pastor and I took it all in, and then asked about the state of her spirit. "How are you holding up?" A wry and confident smile crept across her face. "I'm great," she said. "God is with me and even though we don't know what is going on, he does. My breakthrough is right around the corner."

I remember appreciating her buoyant conviction. I also remember being concerned—what if the breakthrough was further away than she realized? How would the delay impact her faith? Would it hold up? I worried for Laura—but kept the worry to myself. We talked a bit more and prayed for her and left.

Over the course of the next months, we watched in agony as would-be breakthroughs for Laura were quickly followed by crushing setbacks. Each setback not only further confounded the doctors but also battered Laura's buoyancy—confirming my worry. The long trial exacted a heavy toll—decimating her career, her finances, her body, and finally even her confidence in God.

After one particularly devastating setback, I went up to the hospital yet again to visit Laura. The sight of her made me gasp. From a bed in the corner of that sterile hospital room, surrounded by beeping machines and tangled in IV cords, something resembling a corpse greeted me. Laura was now little more than skin and bones; a ninety-pound shadow of a once-vibrant woman. Her appearance shook me.

I steadied myself and entered.

"Laura," I said, "I am so glad to see you."

Was that the right thing to say? I didn't know. No one taught me how to do this in seminary—or anywhere, for that matter. Maybe no one can. Maybe nothing can prepare you for the sight and smell of encroaching death.

"I am glad to see you, too," she replied, doing her best to summon a warm smile as she pushed the words of her greeting through weak lungs, dry mouth, and cracked lips. I pulled up a chair beside her and took her cold hand in mine.

"What's the latest?" I asked. "What are the doctors saying?"

"They still don't have answers," she said. My heart sank.

"And what about you," I asked, fearful of what I might hear. "How are you doing? How are your spirits holding up?"

"I'm exhausted," she replied. "I am tired of being sick. Tired of this broken body. Tired of fighting." My heart broke all over again.

"But mostly," she said, "I am tired of feeling abandoned by God." She gripped my hand and with agony in her voice put hard questions to me. "Andrew," she asked, "Why is this happening? Where is God? Why isn't he doing anything to help me? When is this nightmare going to be over?"

When indeed.

THE CENTER CANNOT HOLD

This is the world we inhabit—a world where urgent questions like the ones posed by Laura burn like embers at the edges of our hearts.

The issues that provoke the questions run the gamut of the human experience, from the national to the international to the very intimate and personal. As I write this, war continues in Gaza and in Ukraine, my country is still wracked by civil and social strife, and even closer to home, the marriages of several dear friends of mine hang in the balance—one false move and lives that have taken decades to build will collapse beyond repair.

Why does it always seem like life teeters on the brink?

As a pastor, I'm deeply aware that examples like these are just the tip of a great iceberg of ache that the Spirit gathers up in our midst when the church assembles on Sundays. "An unquantifiable amount of human pain is about to walk through those doors," I sometimes remind my staff as we prepare for worship. "So be gentle. Life is often hard on these folks, and it is a miracle that many of them are here."

I know this because I know them. I know that they—and perhaps you—are walking in holding the agony of wayward children, of friendships lost to misunderstanding and unforgiveness, of long-buried trauma suddenly blasting through their psychic equilibrium.

I know that they are walking in wracked with anxiety over the loss of jobs, over shifts in the economy that crippled their retirement accounts, over bodies that no longer work as they once did.

I know that behind their brave faces they are fighting back suffocating fears over what they see and hear happening in the streets and city squares, that they are bone-weary from long nights of weeping, that they are constantly throttled by anxious, important questions—will this be the day, the week, the year that the world finally falls apart?

I know these things because I know these people. And because these fears are my fears too. The Irish poet William Butler Yeats described our fears well:

Turning and turning in the widening gyre
The falcon cannot hear the falconer;
Things fall apart; the centre cannot hold.[1]

A cyclone of chaos threatens to rip the world to pieces. Things are falling apart. The center, so it seems, cannot hold. If only the people of God were immune from such things . . .

But we are not. And so we gather for worship and ask with Laura, of our own lives:

Why is this happening?
Where is God?
Why isn't he doing anything to help me?
When is the nightmare going to be over?

What word do we need in such a circumstance? How does the story of Jesus graciously illuminate our chaos and answer our anxious questions?

Welcome to Advent.

HELP IS ON THE WAY

Advent is the monthlong season leading up to Christmas in which we remember that until Christ returns again in glory to judge the living and the dead, we are a *waiting* people.

I first became aware of the meaning of Advent when I was young. My dad, who had a background in theater, offered to stand up in front of the church one Sunday and deliver an a cappella version of the classic hymn "O Come, O Come, Emmanuel." I had never heard the song before and was immediately thunderstruck. Its haunting lines and melody gripped me, and have never left me:

O come, Thou Day-spring, come and cheer
Our spirits by Thine advent here;
Disperse the gloomy clouds of night,
And death's dark shadows put to flight.

That's Advent. It's the season that stares the widening gyre, the unstable center, the gloomy clouds and dark shadows straight in the eye and refuses to blink. Advent stands with us in our recognition that all is not as it should be, and that—the

worst part of it—God, for all we can tell, is often nowhere to
be found. The psalmist gives voice to that recognition:

> How long, LORD? Will you forget me forever?
>   How long will you hide your face from me?
> How long must I wrestle with my thoughts
>   and day after day have sorrow in my heart?
>   How long will my enemy triumph over me?
>   (Psalm 13:1–2)

Four times in two verses, the cry rings out: *How long?* The
problem for the psalmist—as for us—is not just existential.
The problem is theological. The writer expected something
different from life, different from God—and that for good
reason: *God promised it.* The opening move of the psalter set
the expectation:

> Blessed is the one
>   who does not walk in step with the wicked
> or stand in the way that sinners take
>   or sit in the company of mockers,
> but whose delight is in the law of the LORD,
>   and who meditates on his law day and night.
> That person is like a tree planted by streams of water,
>   which yields its fruit in season
> and whose leaf does not wither—
>   whatever they do prospers.
>
> Not so the wicked!
>   They are like chaff
>   that the wind blows away.
> Therefore the wicked will not stand in the judgment,
>   nor sinners in the assembly of the righteous.

For the LORD watches over the way of the righteous,
   but the way of the wicked leads to destruction.
   (Psalm 1)

From God's lips to our ears. We took him at his word. And yet here we are. The fruit *failed*, the leaf *withered*, and the wicked—even the flagrantly wicked—*prosper*. All the evidence of our lives appears to contradict the claim of faith. And to add insult to injury, the God who made such promises seems suddenly to have pulled the rip cord and bailed out on us. Divine indifference bears down upon us like a crushing weight.

We are a resilient species, we human beings. I am constantly astonished by what we can put up with in our relationships with God and one another. Meanness—even very serious meanness—can be overlooked. Cruelties and offenses can be covered over in a spirit of forbearance. Even the deepest betrayals can be forgiven. I have seen it time and time again.

But the one thing no relationship can survive is indifference. Indifference is death. The Holocaust survivor and writer Elie Wiesel once said that the opposite of love is not hate, but *indifference*. If God were angry with us, we could endure it. *Tell us what you're mad about, God, and we'll do our best to make it right*—for anger at least is a sign that despite the disturbance of the moment, the relationship still lives, that we're still *moving toward* each other, that good faith is not finally broken.

But suppose God became indifferent? Suppose the divine heart grew cold, callous, unfeeling? What then? What would become of us?

That is precisely the question that difficulty poses. As in Laura's case, what gives suffering its moral and spiritual urgency is not the pain itself but the question of its *meaning*. Pain can throw us into a place where we experience existence not as a beautiful, fathomless mystery, but as a terrifying, annihilating abyss of un-meaning. The theologian Gustavo Gutiérrez, reflecting on the book of Job, writes that suffering causes Job "to see the universe as chaotic, as lacking the presence of God; from it God is absent as the one who creates it and shapes it into a cosmos."[2] Another poet, W. H. Auden, captured it perfectly. "That is why we despair," he wrote, for

> . . . we are afraid
> Of pain but more afraid of silence; for no nightmare
> Of hostile objects could be as terrible as this Void.
> This is the Abomination. This is the wrath of God.[3]

When the warm summer climes of divine blessing give way to the cruel winter winds of suffering and doubt, we wonder with Job if God has turned his back on us, and in desperation we lift our urgencies to the heavens to see if we can't regain his ear, his heart. "You will call," says Job (reversing the usual biblical formula where *we* call God and *God* answers us), "and I will answer you; you will long for the creature your hands have made" (Job 14:15).

Now just stop and take that in for a moment, friend. Beneath Job's suffering, what he really wants is for God to *want* him again, and Job says so, right to God's face. In so doing he names the deepest desire of every human heart; he cries the cry of every sufferer: Are we seen? Are we known? Are we *wanted*?

We hope so. But we're not sure. Like Job, we vacillate wildly between believing that we are:

> I know that my redeemer lives,
>   and that in the end he will stand on the earth.
> And after my skin has been destroyed,
>   yet in my flesh I will see God;

I myself will see him
with my own eyes—I, and not another.
How my heart yearns within me! (Job 19:25–27)

. . . and despairing of it altogether:

Even if I summoned him and he responded,
I do not believe he would give me a hearing.
He would crush me with a storm
and multiply my wounds for no reason.
He would not let me catch my breath
but would overwhelm me with misery. (Job 9:16–18)

Advent gathers all our doubt and despair, all our vexing questions and soul-crushing anguish, every single last one of our endless, tormented nights and anxious days, acknowledges it, welcomes it, blesses it . . . and then places it all under the word of promise: "Behold, I am coming soon" (Revelation 22:12 ESV).

How soon is *soon*?

We don't know. We aren't told. But of this we are assured:

We are *not* forgotten.
The divine heart has *not* gone cold.
Help is on the way.

A MINI-ADVENT

Our church regularly holds child dedications, a community ritual where we anoint little ones with oil and pray God's blessing over them. Several months ago as we prepared for this time of blessing, we were approached by a couple who serve as foster parents. At the time, they had two little girls—sisters—and a little boy living with them. The boy's situation was particularly bad. His mom had abandoned the family, and his dad had fallen victim to a drug addiction. Removed from these dangerous and chaotic situations, the three children were slowly but surely finding life and strength with their foster parents, and with us.

"We'd like to have the kids dedicated," the couple explained, "but for legal reasons, we can't do it publicly. Would you be willing to gather a few folks together to dedicate them privately after the service?"

Our yes was enthusiastic and immediate. We found a private room in the school where our church worships and gathered a handful of people we trusted to come around the kids to pray. We anointed them with oil, claiming their lives for Jesus and his kingdom. And we pleaded with the God of the orphan and the widow to guard and keep them all their days, restoring their families and them *to* their families if possible, awaking their confidence in Jesus, and finally making us a people capable of carrying their presence with love and wisdom so long as we had them with us.

It was beautiful. And heartrending. *How long will we have them? And when we must finally let them go, will they be safe and loved?*

Merciful Jesus, take pity . . .

In time, the kids were released back to their families. When the little boy was reunited with his dad, who had gotten his addiction under control, the dad was so utterly astonished at the condition that his boy was in that he had to know, just *had* to know: *Who are these people who took such good care of my son?*

Dad soon developed a relationship with the foster parents and then started coming to our church—with the foster parents and with his son for whom we prayed and wept and pled with the God of heaven.

And one Sunday the light broke in and Dad saw: it was *Jesus* who had watched over his son when he could not; it was *Jesus* who had led him successfully through his addiction recovery; it was *Jesus* who had given him new life and a fresh start and a community that treated him and his boy like family; it was *Jesus* who had given him a future; and it was *Jesus* who had given and was giving him hope.

He told us all of this after a service and asked if we would baptize him.

Let me think about it for a minute—YES!

It was one of the most emotional baptisms I've ever been part of. The dad gave his testimony before the entire congregation. Told how Jesus had rescued him. Expressed his everlasting gratitude for how well the community had taken care of his son as he worked to get his life back together. Declared his faith in Jesus. Climbed into the tank and went down into the sacred waters, with his son's foster parents standing on the front row with him in their arms, beaming as they bore witness to an event that for all intents and purposes must be described as *a mini-advent*, a coming of God, a shaft of strange and gracious light that pierced the darkness.

When I lifted the dad out of the waters, the boy leapt from his foster parents' arms and broke into a dead sprint, flinging himself wildly into his father's drenched dripping-wet body and clinging to his neck with a rare, fierce joy. You've never seen anything like it. Not a dry eye in the place.

Behold, I am coming soon . . .

THE COMING(S) OF GOD

I think that story illustrates how the part of the story of Jesus known as Advent works, how its dynamics match the unique dynamics of our experience and how, therefore, it brings us hope, helping us see how our lives, however bleak they may be, under the word of promise can "shine again," as poet Gregory Orr writes, "each object arrayed / In its robe of original light."[4]

Advent re-illuminates what our lives are *really* about, what's *really* going on.

I've learned a great deal about all of this from one of the great theologians of the previous century, Karl Barth. In one of his voluminous works, Barth writes about *parousia*, or what many Christians think of as the "second coming" when Jesus will return. Barth defines *parousia* as "the immediate presence and action of the living Jesus Christ Himself." The time of the church, says Barth, is the time between Christ's first *parousia* and the second.

> [Christ's] first immediate visible presence and action was that in which He encountered the disciples in the forty days after Easter. . . . His second presence and action will be His final coming. . . . The community exists between His coming then as the Risen one and this final coming. Its time is, therefore, this time between.[5]

We live between the "comings" of the Lord, says Barth. Advent teaches us that. It teaches us, as theologian Jürgen Moltmann says, to look forward to the End, to "the still outstanding future of Jesus Christ," a future that "is the ground of the hope which carries faith through the trials of the god-forsaken world and of death."[6]

Amen, I say. "What other time or season can or will the church ever have but that of Advent?" asks Barth.[7] Until Christ returns again in glory to judge the living and the dead, we are a *waiting* people; which means we are an Advent people, living our lives, as priest Fleming Rutledge explains, "on the frontier of the turn of the ages"—a place of "collision," where evil is "most active and most malevolent."[8]

That rings true, doesn't it?

And yet . . .

If we're not careful, the impression we can get from Advent is that *all we have* between the present and the future is waiting on God amid what Moltmann called "the trials of the god-forsaken world and of death."[9] In that case, an Advent faith would be a grim faith, if brave.

But is that really all we have? All Advent gives us?

I don't think so. I think that the Scripture teaches us that our God is active now, mighty to save, which means that we ought to look for and expect the inbreaking of Jesus Christ in our midst, at any time, in any place.

"The decisive difference between a living person and dead one," says Robert Jenson, is that a living person "can *surprise* us as the latter cannot."[10] If the God made known in Jesus Christ is both a "living person" and the Lord of all, then he must be so not just at the *end* of time but to *all times*, which means that *all times* are subject to the divine surprise, that "all occasions are seasons of mercy"[11]—for Christ the Coming One is present to and coming to all of our times.

The twelfth-century Cistercian monk Bernard of Clairvaux said something very much to this effect. In an Advent sermon, Bernard remarked that in addition to the first and second comings of the Lord, there was a third, a "middle coming" in which Jesus Christ "comes in spirit and in power," breaking in amid the trials of a god-forsaken world and of death with life-renewing grace.[12]

Crucially, this too is what Advent teaches, instructing us not only in the fine art of *waiting* and *hoping* that one day all things will be made right, but also (to steal a popular phrase from the world of my religious upbringing—the Pentecostal/charismatic tradition) in the art of *naming* and *claiming* the events of our lives and of our moment in history as acts of divine inbreaking—even where they are not obviously so.

> We take our cue from Jesus himself. In what is now a classic Advent reading, Jesus looks ahead to the coming collapse of Jerusalem. "There will be signs in the sun, moon and stars," he says. "On the earth, nations will be in anguish and perplexity at the roaring and tossing of the sea. People will faint from terror, apprehensive of what is coming on the world, for the heavenly bodies will be shaken. At that time they will see the Son of Man coming in a cloud with power and great glory. When these things begin to take place, stand up and lift up your heads, because your redemption is drawing near" (Luke 21:25–28).

Now that is remarkable—a powerful example of how the story of Jesus changes how we see. Where some will see nothing but collapse and calamity, Jesus says the faithful will see a *coming* of the Messiah to make all things new. What looks like breakdown to some will look like *breakthrough* to the eyes of faith. So, Jesus says, when the world seems to be spinning out of control, "stand up and lift up your heads, because your redemption is drawing near."

That is to say, *Even at what feels like the very end of the world, look for me, for I am there, present to bless and renew your life.*

As a pastor, I find all of this incredibly helpful. Advent teaches me to speak "Jesus" with the full force and authority of the biblical witness, to any and every situation the person in front of me may be in—including you, friend.

When tears fall from Laura's agonized, weary eyes, I can say, "Behold, the coming of God . . ." When parents once mired in drug addiction are reunited with their kids, I can say, "Behold, the coming of God . . ." And when it feels like the world we once knew is buckling and heaving and falling into the annihilating abyss and none of us has the power to arrest that fall, we can say, and say boldly, "Behold, the coming of God . . ." because in Christ, God has come and is coming and will come again.

So, yeah, Karl, we're with you:

It's all Advent.

WAITING WITH GOD FOR GOD

And so, amid all the trials and tribulations of the present age, we wait on God; for his full and final inbreaking, we wait—as the psalmist said, "More than watchmen wait for the morning" (Psalm 130:6).

It isn't easy. The road we travel is long and difficult, and full of danger. The philosopher and Jesuit priest Pierre Teilhard de Chardin put it perfectly in one of his prayers:

Above all, trust in the slow work of God.
We are quite naturally impatient in everything to reach
    the end without delay.
We should like to skip the intermediate stages.
We are impatient of being on the way to something
    unknown, something new.

And yet it is the law of all progress
that it is made by passing through some stages of instability—
and that it may take a very long time.[13]

Yes, it may. And usually does.

Why our God chooses to do things this way—taking a long time, acting in large part in hidden and secret ways—is beyond our ken. There are tantalizing hints and suggestions scattered throughout Scripture. Peter wrote that "the Lord is not slow in keeping his promise, as some understand slowness. Instead he is patient with you, not wanting anyone to perish, but everyone to come to repentance" (2 Peter 3:9). Some great, cosmic work, Peter tells us, is on the line, and were God to rush the process, plucking the fruit before it is ripe, the great good he has planned would be lost.

And rest assured, it is a *great* good: "Eye has not seen, nor ear heard, nor has it entered into the heart of man the things which God has prepared" (1 Corinthians 2:9 MEV). Or as Paul wrote elsewhere: "Now to him who is able to do immeasurably more than all we ask or imagine" (Ephesians 3:20).

His plans outpace our asking and exceed our imagining. And he is prepared to wait "a very long time" to see them come to pass.

And, therefore, so must we. We wait for God . . .

But not for an *absent* God. Christ the Coming One is still and always our Immanuel, as Barth writes, "by the Holy Spirit . . . invisibly present as the Living Head in the midst of His Body"[14]—yet here and there making himself visible to the eyes of faith, and thereby becoming, according to Bernard, "our rest and consolation," his presence in our midst "like a road on which we travel from the first coming to the last."[15] Or as Catherine of Sienna put it: "All the way to heaven is heaven because Christ is the way."[16]

We are thus like Simeon at the temple in another classic Advent text: "He was waiting for the consolation of Israel, *and the Holy Spirit was on him*" (Luke 2:25, emphasis added).

As a people of the Spirit, we wait *with* God *for* God.

Chapter 1
QUESTIONS FOR DISCUSSION

1. What has Advent meant to you on your spiritual
    journey? How has this chapter challenged or filled
    out that meaning?

2. Can you think of a time in your life when you experi-
    enced a "mini-Advent"?

3. How have you handled seasons of waiting? What has
    it looked like for you to wait *with* God *for* God?

2

CHRISTMAS

Everything Holy

The Word became flesh . . .
—JOHN 1:14

You know how it is when some great king enters a large
city and dwells in one of its houses . . . because of his
dwelling in that single house, the whole city is honored.
—SAINT ATHANASIUS, *On the Incarnation*

Holiness has a way of ambushing you. It's happened to me
many times. Often in places I would least expect it.

On a Tuesday evening in the summer of 2006, my wife
Mandi had been in labor for the better part of a night and
a day. After thirty-six grueling hours she finally (and safely,
thank God) delivered a twenty-one-and-a-half inch, nine-
pound, ten-ounce chunk of humanity: our oldest son, Ethan.
Did I mention he was large? When he landed in the lap of the
doctor who delivered him, she held him aloft and turned to
Mandi and exclaimed, "This is a *huge* baby!"—as if that were
news to Mandi, who, all her joy notwithstanding, was mostly

grateful to have the excessively large infant out, ravenous for a good meal and a long sleep to heal her exhausted body.

She got both. And as the clock neared midnight, with my bride of six years sleeping peacefully in the bed beside me, I suddenly found myself alone with my newborn son, cleaned and clothed and wrapped in blankets and resting comfortably in my arms. Our first father-son moments together. *What do I do now?* I wondered.

I did what comes natural to me as a preacher: I started talking to him. First about us—his mom and dad—and what we're like. About how much he was going to enjoy living with us. About how much we'd looked forward to having him in our lives.

Next, I started telling him about our families. About who they were and what they were like. About not just *where* but *who* we came from. About our now deeply intertwined histories and the blood that ran in his veins—what he was heir to.

The family storytelling came in for a landing, and I began to talk to him about God. About the One who hung the sun and the stars and holds it all—him included—in the palm of his hands. About how much God loved him, how God would do anything for him, and how one day he would come to know that. I told my son about how the love of God would touch his heart like it had touched ours, and how that day would be the best day.

Before I knew it—and to my great surprise—I was weeping. Profusely. The Presence had fallen, blindsiding me with God—ambushing me with holiness.

I began to pray, fervently pray, the Lord's protection and blessing over Ethan; and then, wiping my eyes, I made the sign of the cross on his forehead with those same tears. It felt like I was baptizing my son in a Jordan River of fatherly ache.

The intensity of it all—I remember so well—was so very startling and sudden. A tsunami of emotion, which after a half hour so began to subside—a tide of Presence going back out to sea. I concluded the prayer, laid Ethan in his bassinet, stretched out on the couch, and with a strong sense of God still lingering in the room, fell into a deep, happy sleep.

EVERYTHING THAT IS

Looking back years later, what strikes me about that encounter—even more than the sheer intensity of it—is my own surprise about it. I had simply not *expected* God in a place like that.

Which is odd because I was raised in church. I'd experienced God powerfully in dozens of worship services across the years, and more times than I could possibly have counted in private prayer. Those moments—all of them—shaped me.

But rarely to that point in my life had I experienced God in places like the one just described: in a hospital room, in a tender, oh-so-human moment, in the encounter of *bodies* with one another. It stunned me, that moment did, not just for its *immensity*, but for its *location*. I count the experience a deep and lasting sign of the Mercy in my life, for it taught me much that I needed to know about God.

It is still teaching me. And, as a pastor, I am trying to teach others.

When the church calendar turns from the waiting of Advent to the joy of Christmas, what suddenly comes into focus is what Christians have called "the incarnation"—the event in which, as Eugene Peterson puts it so beautifully in his translation of John 1:14, "The Word became flesh and blood, *and moved into the neighborhood*" (*The Message*, emphasis added).

The incarnation—the "enfleshment"—of God in the person of Jesus is the touchstone of Christian faith. Everything we have to say about the nature of redemption depends upon it, pivots around it. We have no Christianity without the Word-in-flesh, without God-in-a-body. As one of the teachers of the early church, Tertullian, put it, *Caro salutis est cardo*: the flesh— Jesus' flesh—is the hinge of the whole enterprise of salvation.[1] Karl Barth agrees: "'God with us' is the centre of the Christian message."[2] All that God intends to do for us he does through this—through the miracle sung and celebrated at Christmas.

But just *what* is that miracle? What does it mean for us? How does it change how we see?

I have become convinced that however much we may love Christmas, the garden variety believer—including many a pastor—misses the depth and breadth of its significance. What C. S. Lewis called "the great miracle"[3] is reduced to a curiosity at best, a pious irrelevance at worst. And that is a tragedy.

"Everything that lives," says the poet William Blake, "is holy."[4] I concur. But in the name of the One who became incarnate for us and for our salvation, I believe that we should draw the circle wider, expand the circumference of holiness.

"Everything that *is*," I say, "is holy." There is not an inch of the cosmos that is not saturated with holiness. Not on its own merit, but because God has made it holy, including it in and sanctifying it by the Presence.

Christians can say such things with confidence about the cosmos because of the story they tell. About how once upon a time, in a cave outside Bethlehem, God came. A human baby, born to a young woman—just a teenager—mewling and wet and hungry, surrounded by animals, turns out to have been nothing less than the "God-with-us" of which Barth spoke.

In Jesus, God came. Holiness entered the world—in a human body, as a human body.

And that moving-in *does something* to the world—something that cannot be undone.

Every December, as part of my spiritual preparation for Christmas, I return to one of my favorite choral pieces: the American composer Morten Lauridsen's *O magnum mysterium*. It takes my breath away. Every time. Sung in Latin, the English translation is as follows:

O great mystery,
and wonderful sacrament,
that animals should see the newborn Lord,
lying in a manger!
Blessed is the virgin whose womb
was worthy to bear
the Lord, Jesus Christ.
Alleluia![5]

Advent told us that God was *coming*. Christmas tells us that God *came*, in this most miraculous and notorious way—that somehow, remaining what he was, the Second Person of the Trinity was knit of our flesh and slipped into the world under the cover of darkness to live as one of us and sanctify the whole creation in the process. As theologian Kathryn Tanner explains, God "freely wishes to replicate to every degree possible [his] fullness of life, light, and love outward in what is not God; this is possible," she goes on, "only to the extent that the world is united by God to Godself."[6] And that's what Christians believe has happened in the incarnation of Jesus—the world has been united to God, God replicating the fullness of God's life in what is not God.

And that—by the way—is the power of nativity art. It's not just that the Christ-child is full of light, but that light streams *from* the Christ-child, lighting everything up around him. Later in the Gospels, even the clothes that Jesus wears on the Mount of Transfiguration are made supernaturally bright by the light that he is and has. This whole weary world is caught up in the transfiguring light of the incarnation of the One whom the Nicene Creed—one of the most ancient statements of Christian faith—calls "God from God, Light from Light."

Because of Jesus, everything that is, is holy.

KISS THE EARTH

But we are slow to see this. And our lives are the poorer as a result.

The form of Christianity I was raised in tended to prioritize the "spiritual" over the material.[7] Worship services and Bible reading and times of private prayer were therefore seen as the primary places of divine encounter. Everything else—really, most of "normal" life: life in bodies and in homes and in neighborhoods—took a back seat.

We had a view of the end times to match that prioritizing of the spiritual over the material: one day the Lord Jesus would return to take the faithful *out of* their bodies to live with him somewhere *other than* here, in this beautiful if broken world that God had made. Bodies were therefore (at best) incidental to or (at worst) hindrances to life with God—even though, as Gustavo Gutiérrez points out, to the biblical mind, "the body is not something the human person *has*, but something it *is*." Even though it is true that our bodies, our *lives*, are places where "death-dealing power operates," it is precisely in those same places that "the Spirit, the power that gives life, is also active."[8] Our *bodies* are always the locus of salvation.

Which is why, for example, the Nicene Creed ends not with a hope for escape but for "the resurrection of the dead and the life of the world to come." As another theologian, Catherine LaCugna, puts it, because of the incarnation our *bodies* have become partakers of the *imago Dei*, the image of God (that is, Jesus), with the result that "it is the *body* that is raised on the last day."[9] One day, Scripture teaches, the Presence of God will so supersaturate our world that every dead thing will rise, the cosmos in its furthest reaches transfigured by the Light and Life of the God to whom we are united in Jesus, the Incarnate One.

But I was well into my twenties before I knew any of that, for the mentality was deeply ingrained in me. It took an act of God to begin to uproot it.

When I was a sophomore in college, newly married and beginning to feel my way around a life of adult responsibility, I decided one morning to wake up a bit earlier than normal to try to get a jump on the day.

The alarm went off at five. I had expected to be groggy, but for some reason I was lucid. Very lucid. My plan was to start the morning with a little prayer and then head out on a run before getting cleaned up for the day. If I had time, I thought I might head to a nearby coffee shop to grab a cup before class.

From the first, the air crackled with a sense of Presence. I drank deeply of it in prayer, grateful for the gift, and expected it to subside as I wrapped up my time of devotion and entered the day's tasks—the "normal" stuff, you know? Where God *is not*.

Strangely, that sense of Presence did not subside—it intensified.

I don't quite know how to describe what the next few hours were like except to say that they were ecstasy. Pure, unmitigated ecstasy. Every step of my run in the cool fall air felt like an act of adoration. Showering and drying off and pulling old jeans and a warm sweater over my body felt like worship. Driving to and from the coffee shop felt like an act of gratitude for the sheer gift of life. A cataract of "thank you's" cascaded effortlessly off my lips for three hours. It was a euphoric experience of God—again, *in the stuff of normal life*. And it changed everything for me.

There's a moment in Dostoevsky's novel *The Brothers Karamazov* when the elderly monk Father Zossima says to his listeners,

> Love to throw yourself on the earth and kiss it. Kiss the earth and love it with an unceasing, consuming love. Love all men, love everything. Seek that rapture and ecstasy. Water the earth with the tears of your joy and love those tears. Don't be ashamed of that ecstasy, prize it, for it is a gift of God and a great one.[10]

That day in the fall of my sophomore year I could have done just that; I could have fallen down in the dirt and embraced it and wept for the way it conveyed God to me, the way it became a place of communion, a vehicle of Presence. "A hundred times through the fields and along the deep roads," writes Annie Dillard, "I've cried Holy."[11] That happened to me that day, for the very first time (and thankfully not for the last).

And there also for the first time I saw the divine value of all things, beheld the Holy Depth at the heart of all life.

The experience changed how I read Scripture. Suddenly I saw the whole story as a story of sacred Presence, of God's determination to hold communion with us in the temple of his creation. A story culminating in the coming of the

Presence-in-flesh who taught us to pray that his Father's name would be hallowed here on earth, in all the stuff of ordinary living, just like it is in heaven. A story of God-with-us, and all things hallowed by the self-hallowing of the Name which has come to rest among us in Jesus Christ.

It also changed how I looked at creation and things and people. The whole cosmos became for me like the garden of Eden where God walked in the cool of the day (Genesis 3:8). Things—food and drink and money and possessions—became gifts from the Father of heavenly lights, meant to be cherished and enjoyed in accordance with God's purpose for them (James 1:17). And people became unspeakably precious manifestations of the divine image, icons of God endowed with infinite dignity, destined for glory.

And I saw also that personal holiness—all the moral and spiritual rectitude of our lives—must surely consist in this: living aligned with that truth.

That is, the truth of the incarnation.

LOVE YOUR LIFE

For all the good my tradition gave me (and it gave me much good), its habit of pivoting away from incarnational faith was a very deep error, which the Spirit has and is mercifully correcting in me.

But I have come to see that such errors are really not unique to my tribe. Crack open the books of church history, and you'll see that the temptation to degrade the world of "things" has dogged our steps from the very first, telling us that we must spurn the conditions of our createdness and indeed our very lives—the lives God has given us so that we might know and love him—in favor of something higher, better, more sublime, more spiritual, if we hope to find God. In the first few centuries of the church, these people were sometimes known as the "gnostics" for their tendency to denigrate material reality. Their philosophy, gnosticism, still lives—though not always by that name. Whatever form it takes, gnosticism is always trying to take us away from God-with-us in our actual lives to *somewhere else*. And our lives are crippled with sadness as a result.

It causes me deep pain as a pastor to see folks live this way. But it happens all the time. In so many different ways.

I once pastored a man who had lost his wife a decade before we met. The two had had a long and happy marriage before she was diagnosed with dementia. The period of her decline was grueling. And then she passed. A year of grieving turned into two turned into ten for her husband. Despite being surrounded by friends and family and the good gifts of God, in ten years he had not shifted in any direction but sadness. His grief seemed only to have solidified rather than softened into space where seeds of hope and joy could sprout into new life. After spending much time with him in counsel and prayer, I began to wonder whether he simply did not *want* to. During one of our times together, he said, "I can't wait for Jesus to come back and get me out of here."

I sighed. He believed that God was *somewhere else* for him. I heard his heart—how often I have thought similar thoughts in times of sadness—but I couldn't have disagreed more.

My wife and I sat with a woman in our church who wanted to leave her husband and family. Twenty years into a family story, she suddenly decided she needed *out*. We were perplexed, so we asked: *Has your husband been abusive? Unfaithful? Untrustworthy?* No—she just felt constricted and unhappy by the shape of their lives and was convinced that a change of scenery would do the trick.

She believed that God was *somewhere else* for her. We couldn't have disagreed more.

Those, of course, are extreme examples. But more commonly I see the ennui that many people carry around as a permanent psychological atmosphere, a vague and chronic boredom with life. Nothing really moves them. "We played the pipe for you, and you did not dance; we sang a dirge, and you did not mourn" (Matthew 11:17). And yet they hold fast to the thought that if things were different, they would have joy.

They think, in other words, that God is *somewhere else* for them. I couldn't disagree more.

I want to shout at them with the words of Mary Oliver: "If you have not been enchanted by this adventure—your life— what would do for you?"[12] And with Henry David Thoreau: "However mean your life is, meet and live it; do not shun it and call it hard names . . . The fault-finder will find faults even in paradise. Love your life, poor as it is."[13] The notion of a "somewhere else" where we will *really* find God is a delusion and a snare. In nearly twenty years of ministry, I've come to believe that no small part of my job as a pastor is to help put people *back in their lives* so that they might see them as places of communion, of Presence. My work is to help them see that the whole entire thing—marriage and sex and work and play and singleness and friendship and eating and drinking and paying the bills and doing the chores and tending to little ones and visiting aging grandparents and fishing and climbing mountains and making art and making friends and listening to music and watching movies and reading great books and savoring a great cup of coffee *as well as* showing up for corporate worship and seeking God in the silences of the heart—that all of it is (to use theologian John Webster's memorable phrase) "the domain of the Word,"[14] a place of God's Presence, because the Word has come among us and made a home here.

That's what being a people of the incarnation is all about. It's about believing that since everything is shot through with the divine Presence, everywhere is potentially a place of communion, and that at any time, we may be gobsmacked by Holiness when we least expect it.

ANOTHER ENCOUNTER

I came home from an appointment one day to this greeting from Mandi: "You need to go out and check the back alley. Someone's out there and I think something is seriously wrong with him."

I didn't dare ask why she hadn't gone out to check. In fact, I was glad she hadn't. We were new church planters living just outside a major urban center, in a rough and rundown area of the city, with three toddlers. The *pop-pop* of gunfire, the sound of high-speed police chases, and the sight of sketchy characters wandering our neighborhood at all hours of the day and night had become our new normal. I constantly worried about the safety of my family.

"Okay," I said, taking a deep breath and grabbing a bag of trash (I felt I needed a pretext for heading into the alley, and throwing away some trash seemed like a reasonable one) and went out the back door, dreading and bracing myself for what I might find.

When I opened the gate, I saw a man in his forties covered in vomit and crumpled up next to the dumpster with a mostly empty bottle of Kentucky Deluxe in his hand. He reeked of alcohol and cigarettes and puke, and I honestly couldn't tell whether he was alive or dead. So I did the only thing I could think to do (feels like a recurring problem for me, eh?): I started talking.

"Hello," I said.

Somewhat to my astonishment, he looked up at me and responded with a slurred and half-lucid grunt acknowledging my presence; and with that, a conversation began—one that I was wildly unprepared for.

I asked what was, to me anyway, the obvious next question: "Are you okay?" He began to explain that he had panhandled all day and bought the bourbon and, you know, overdid it a bit with the result that this vomit over here and . . . you get the point.

This was all very new for me. I was born into a white middle-class family, and to that point, I had spent most of my life in "decent" neighborhoods. Outside of a few service days at local homeless shelters, I had never really interacted with a person who lived on the streets—least of all in an uncontrolled environment. My anxiety, as you can imagine, was high.

I walked over toward the dumpster (and him) to throw my trash away. "Rough day," I said. "Are you hungry?" He admitted that he was, and so I went back into the house to pack him a bag of food—a sandwich and an apple and some brownies Mandi had just made.

When I returned with the food, he was ready to talk. He stood to his feet to receive the little lunch we had packed, and a stream of words began to pour out of his mouth. He explained that his name was Dave and that he had lived here his whole life and had helped build the house we were living in (which didn't quite make sense, since the house was more than a hundred years old). He told me about his family and his life and how he had wound up on the street and so on for what felt like a very long time, until I finally became uncomfortable and tried to bail out of the conversation with a rather sanctimonious "Dave, can I pray for you?"

"Of course," he said. I put my hand on his shoulder (keeping his foul-smelling and—in my mind anyway—potentially dangerous body a safe and manageable distance from my own), prayed a polite, quick prayer, and was just about to head through the alley gate when Dave asked if he could return the favor.

"Umm . . . sure," I replied. Before I even knew what was happening, Dave had wrapped his arm around me, pulled my body close to his own, and through a mouthful of busted teeth and barf-ridden bourbon-and-tobacco breath, with utter sincerity, prayed for God's blessing and favor on my life and the life of my family.

And do you know what happened? The Presence rushed in. The same Presence I'd felt in prayer and worship. The same Presence I'd felt that morning in college. The same Presence I'd felt when I held my oldest in my arms for the first time.

Darndest thing.

It staggered me more than all those moments combined. That there in a filthy back alley in front of a dumpster, the hands, arms, and body of this man, bullied and bruised by life, had somehow become a vehicle for the Presence.

NO ORDINARY PEOPLE

I was dumbfounded. But maybe I shouldn't have been. Maybe I should have just paid closer attention to the story. The story of how the God's coming in a human body dignifies and elevates not just every *thing* but every *body*. "You know how it is when some great king enters a large city and dwells in one of its houses," says Saint Athanasius, "because of his dwelling in that single house, the whole city is honored."[15]

To the Christian mind, bodies, all bodies, are sacred and must be treated—honored—as such. This is one of the great gifts we give the world. Helping people come to grips with that sacredness is central to our evangelistic task.

The body, of course, has become a great problem in our day. The culture around us seems ever more incapable of speaking a clear or coherent word on its purpose and value. Which is a problem, because so much depends on the value we place on the body—whether we are talking about sexuality, public policy about the treatment of immigrants and refugees, or what it might look like to continue building justice and peace between people of different ethnic and social backgrounds. When the world talks the body, it struggles for solid footing.

So it is worth wondering—what precisely can the church say about the body, why can we say it (that is, what grounds it?), and how ought we to say it?

Where the culture does not have clear answers, Christian faith does. Funded by what it knows about the world now that the Son of God has become one of us, the church is bold to say that bodies are fashioned in the image and likeness of God (Genesis 1:26–27). It says that they are an admixture of the material and mystical (Genesis 2:7), poised at the intersection between heaven and earth, our roots pushing deep into clay even as the branches of our hearts stretch out and up to the heavens.

It says further, astonishingly, that One of the Trinity came in a body, *as* a body, and lived and died as one of us. Because of that One, it says, our bodies are temples of the Holy Spirit (1 Corinthians 6:19) and purposed for full and final union with God (1 Corinthians 6:13).

Human bodies therefore have absolute sacred value; our finite flesh is infinitely cherished by infinite God. C. S. Lewis said it perhaps better than anyone:

> It is a serious thing to live in a society of possible gods and goddesses, to remember that the dullest most uninteresting person you can talk to may one day be a creature which, if you saw it now, you would be strongly tempted to worship . . . it is with the awe and the circumspection proper to [this] that we should conduct all of our dealings with one another, all friendships, all loves, all play, all politics. There are no ordinary people. You have never talked to a mere mortal . . . it is immortals whom we joke with, work with, marry, snub, and exploit.[16]

Christian faith is a long training in the awe and circumspection of which Lewis spoke—a learned reverence for all God has made us to be, all he has done for us in the body of the man who was God, Jesus the Christ.

As a pastor, I think about this often. In a time when cities are being carpet-bombed, when families are being separated at borders, when the unborn are being killed by the tens of thousands each year, and when so many are doing damage to their bodies in the name of so-called beauty or happiness, and when ethnic strife still rages around the world, what do Christians do?

I will tell you.

In the name of the One who took our broken, sin-desecrated bodies and re-sacralized them by his coming in flesh:

We treat our bodies with respect and dignity.
We care for the orphan and the widow.
We welcome the stranger at the gate.
We visit the sick and suffering and dying.

We tend to the prisoner and outcast.
We baptize and anoint our children in the Name.
We work hard to honor and include the physically disabled
and those with special needs.
We cherish the poor.

In short, we receive one another as Jesus Christ himself,
knowing that because of the incarnation, *whenever we deal
with people, we deal with God.*

Chapter 2

QUESTIONS FOR DISCUSSION

1. How did this chapter deepen or challenge your understanding of the incarnation?

2. In what ways has your religious tradition conditioned you to experience the Presence of God in some places and not others? How has the Spirit corrected that in you?

3. What might it look like in your own life to reclaim the dignity of the body?

3

EPIPHANY

A Great Light

The people living in darkness have seen a great light.
—**MATTHEW 4:16**

My subject in fiction is the action of grace in territory
held largely by the devil.
—**FLANNERY O'CONNOR**, *Mystery and Manners*

The Son of God takes on flesh, moving into the world under the cover of darkness to sanctify and save it. "Like a thief in the night" is how Paul said Jesus would return at the consummation of the ages (1 Thessalonians 5:2), and I suspect that such is the case because that is how he most typically comes—the divine incognito.

God, it seems to me, enjoys being unnoticed; and most of his work is, in fact, unnoticed. Isaiah recognized this: "Truly, you are a God who hides himself, O God of Israel, the Savior" (Isaiah 45:15 ESV). The great majority of God's doings are out of our sight. We catch "but the outer fringe of his works" (Job 26:14).

The divine preference for obscurity notwithstanding, revelation—that is, *epiphany*—is critical to the Story. The Father reveals the Son to the world. The mission to redeem the cosmos depends upon it. "I will . . . make you a light to the nations" (Isaiah 49:6 MEV). If Advent told us that the Light was coming, and Christmas told us that in Christ it had come, the season that follows next, Epiphany, opens our eyes to the *point* of the Coming—to the identity and the work of the One who lights up the world.

"The people living in darkness have seen a great light," writes Matthew (in 4:16, quoting Isaiah), and then shows us just what happens when the "great light" dawns:

> Jesus went throughout Galilee, teaching in their synagogues, proclaiming the good news of the kingdom, and healing every disease and sickness among the people. News about him spread all over Syria, and people brought to him all who were ill with various diseases, those suffering severe pain, the demon-possessed, those having seizures, and the paralyzed; and he healed them. Large crowds from Galilee, the Decapolis, Jerusalem, Judea and the region across the Jordan followed him. (Matthew 4:23–25)

Small wonder "large crowds" followed him. Of course they did. He made their lives right—teaching, healing, and casting out demons wherever he went.

And as it was then, so it is now. When Jesus, the Light, comes among us, he teaches, and heals, and drives back the darkness.

TEACHING AS ONE HAVING AUTHORITY

The most notable feature of the life of Jesus may be his role as a teacher. Talk to the garden-variety nonbeliever today about him, and they'll almost invariably mention the respect they have for his teaching.

And why shouldn't they? The teachings of Jesus comprise so much of the text of the Gospels, and their genius is undeniable. In John, the crowds marvel, "How did this man get such learning without having been taught?" (John 7:15). But it's more than just genius. As Matthew, Mark, and Luke are so apt to note, Jesus taught "as one having authority" (Matthew 7:29 et al. NKJV). His words had, and have, power, authority. The truth of his teaching commands assent.

During my seminary years, I worked as a host at a restaurant. One day in the middle of a shift, one of my fellow hosts—a young woman attending a local Jesuit university who had no real religious background and who knew that I was preparing for ministry—said to me, "You have to study the Bible in seminary, right?"

"Yep." I said, "Why do you ask?"

"Well," she explained, "my university is making me take a class on the Gospels. I've never read them before. If I've got questions as I go along, would you mind answering them?"

"Happy to," I said.

Several weeks went by before we worked another shift together. "How's the class on the Gospels going?" I asked.

"Great," she replied. "We're studying that place right at the beginning of Matthew where Jesus does a bunch of teaching."

"The Sermon on the Mount?" I asked.

"Yeah, that's it," she said.

"Well, what do you think?" I was curious to know how these words—which I'd been reading all my life—were coming across to someone encountering them for the first time.

"It's really incredible," she replied. "Like, you know that place where Jesus says if you don't cheat on your spouse but kind of do it in your heart, it's basically like the same thing?"

"Yeah," I said.

"*I've always believed that!*"

That made me smile.

"Really?" I said.

"Yeah," she went on, "and the more I read of Jesus, the more I find myself thinking, *He's right . . . he's right . . . how can he be so right?!*"

I swear you can't make this stuff up.

"That's really cool," I said. "I'll tell you something. I've been reading Jesus' words my whole life, and I can almost guarantee you this: that if you keep this up, you'll come to a point where your thoughts will shift from "*He's right . . .*" to "*He must be more than just a man . . .*"

She paused to take that in. And then this:

"I think that's already starting to happen."

Unbelievable.

As one having authority . . .

There's a tendency in our day—in Christianity no less than in other religions—to blunt and soften the sharper edges of our teaching. Some years ago I walked into a local coffee shop and saw a flyer on a bulletin board that read, "Judaism Your Way!" It was an advertisement for a local synagogue whose ministry was under significant reconstruction to try to reach new people. I remember thinking, "This is a bad idea. Judaism *your way* is the very last thing Judaism is. Judaism is the religion of Moses and the prophets. The religion that, in the name of Yahweh, Lord of heaven and earth, has from time immemorial called judgment down on kings and kingdoms, shaking the heavens and the earth. Its difference, its *oddity*, is part of its point. More than that, it is part of its *power*. If you lose that, you lose all."

The same is true of Christianity. The oddity of our Teacher is part of the point. Part of the power. We do no one a service by hiding it.

A man started coming to my church awhile back who was a self-confessed atheist. "Pastor," he said after a service, "I am here because there's a woman in your congregation I'd like to date. She told me she won't date non-Christians, but that I'd be welcome to come to church with her. I like her and want to spend time with her. So, here I am."

I laughed. The honesty was refreshing. "Great," I said. "It's good to have you here. Is there anything I can do for you?"

"Well," he replied, "I figure while I'm here, I might as well learn something about what she believes. Can you recommend some books?"

"Yep," I said, and went on to recommend some stuff by C. S. Lewis and N. T. Wright and several others I thought might be helpful, along with a Bible—a good, stiff drink of Jesus, as it were. A few months went by before we spoke again after one of our services.

"Pastor," he said, "I've been reading those books."

"Great," I replied. "What do you think?"

"They're interesting," he said. "Especially the Bible."

"Oh really? What do you think about *that*?"

"Honestly, I can't make heads or tails of it . . ." he said. And then went on: "*Can you tell me what the Bible is about?*"

Again. Seriously.

I took a deep breath and gave him the basic plot of the Bible, such as I understand it. A good world gone bad because of sin. God's effort to make it right in the person of Jesus. The promise that one day Jesus and his Father will make all things new. That kind of thing.

"Huh," he said. "I appreciate it."

He kept coming to worship, singing and sometimes saying the Nicene Creed with us, hearing me prattle on and on about Jesus—about his life and his teaching and his triumph over sin and death and how he was somehow mysteriously present in bread and cup . . . trying to make sense of it all. I knew it struck him as strange. *Because it is strange.* All of it. I loved that he was with us and pressing into the strangeness.

After a few months, we spoke again after a service.

"Pastor," he said, "I think I need to get baptized."

"Oh yeah," I replied, "why is that?"

"Because you know that part of the service where you all stand up and say the stuff that you believe?"

"The Nicene Creed?" I asked.

"Yeah that. Well, a couple weeks ago I was standing with you guys saying the Creed and suddenly it dawned on me: *I believe this . . . all of this . . . this is my faith too . . .*"

I started laughing. Jesus did it again.

He taught as one having authority . . .

(Oh, and he did wind up marrying the woman. God is good.)

PERFORMING HEALINGS AND SIGNS

If teaching is the most notable feature of the ministry of Jesus, surely the healings are a close second. From the downbeat all the way to the end of his life, Jesus healed.

The healings raise a critical question for us: Does the presence of God in Jesus make any tangible difference for the world that you and I inhabit *today*? If so, what's the difference?

In the circles I was raised in, we were taught to believe that the presence of God in Jesus made *all* the difference in the world; that because Jesus was the same "yesterday and today and forever" (Hebrews 13:8), he could, and did, still heal—as he did in the Gospels. We therefore expected, and saw, miracles.

When I was training for ministry, I was surprised to learn that not every tradition of Christian faith believed this. In fact, many, I came to find out, were skeptical of it and had built theologies to justify and institutionalize their skepticism. They taught their people that faith was mostly a matter of spiritual and moral renewal; as for miracles, since they no longer occurred, it was misguided to seek them.

I tried to follow their arguments, but when I did, I found they made hopeless nonsense out of the Bible. What is more, I found they led to a web of contradictions that bordered on outright hypocrisy.

When I was in seminary, our classes often ended with prayer requests. At the end of Greek class one day, a hand went up: "A dear friend of my family has been diagnosed with a stage four brain tumor," he said. "It's inoperable. His family is reeling. I'd be grateful if we could pray for healing."

Our professor asked who might be willing to pray, and another hand went up. The prayer, which I will never forget, went something like this:

> Dear God, thank you that you are sovereign over all things, that no plan of yours can be thwarted, and that this tumor did not catch you by surprise. We thank you for the peace and comfort that gives us. We pray that peace and comfort would fall upon this family, and especially upon this beloved child of yours who now has only a little while to live. Surround them all with your presence. Let them know that they are loved, and that you are holding them and all their days in the palm of your hand. In the name of Jesus, we pray. Amen.

A pious prayer—and ghastly. I looked around to see whether anyone else was appalled too. Not only did the prayer strike me as very bad manners (the specific request was healing from the brain tumor, which did not get prayed for), it was also logically absurd. *Even the granting of a sense of peace and comfort involves an act of God*; that is to say, a divine intervention—which is, of course, *a miracle*. If it is not too difficult for God to do whatever it is God must do to grant a sense of comfort, surely it is not any *more* difficult for God to touch and dissolve a brain tumor. Which is why I say that the failure to pray for healing—opting for peace and comfort instead—is illogical. Both are acts of God.

Sometimes we act and speak like there are *degrees* of difficulty for God. That tumors are more challenging for the divine being than positive feelings. But surely that makes us pagans rather than Christians, believers in the gods rather than the God who reveals himself in creation and covenant and, above all, in Jesus Christ, the Healer. "Behold, I am the LORD, the God of all flesh," says this One on the lips of Jeremiah, "is anything too difficult for Me?" (Jeremiah 32:27 NASB).

How we answer that question matters.

I think we pray prayers like the one my classmate prayed because we are afraid of being disappointed. It's easier, and safer, to hedge our bets. I understand that. I do. The disappointment is real. For as many times as I have seen the hoped-for healing come to pass, I have also seen it *not* come to pass. It can be, and often is, crushing. I, too, have sat by the bedside of dying loved ones and wept and prayed and cried out for healing, only to bury them a week later.

I don't have an explanation for that—for why God heals some and not others. No one does. And the ones who *try* to offer explanations wind up hurting people by telling them that it was a lack of faith or hidden sin that "blocked" their healing.

God, forgive us for that. For weaponizing your gifts.

All the same, I take it to be an act of bad faith bordering on mutiny to fail, when the moment calls for it, to cry out to the living God for healing—if for no other reason than because Jesus told us to pray for the sick (Matthew 10:8 et al.) and because the Bible commands it (James 5:15).

Even so, we have more reason to pray for healing than just blind obedience. For what is really at stake—and here is the urgency of the matter—is our view of God. Is God active in the world to make it right, or not? Or is he just letting it all burn before the Great Renewal? Does Redemption touch our *actual* lives, or is it forever locked up in the world of the Bible or in the future that God will one day bring, at an impossible remove from our own?

St. Augustine is helpful here. After painstakingly documenting several miraculous healings in his masterpiece, *The City of God*, Augustine remarks that the miracles occurred "to testify to that one supreme miracle of salvation, the miracle of Christ's ascension into heaven *in the flesh in which he rose from the dead.*"[1]

For Augustine, however much the miracles were certainly discrete acts of divine compassion on the sufferer, they were also much more than that—they were testimonies to the whole will of God for human life; namely, that in Christ our whole humanity is healed and carried up to the heavens, deified (more on how the ascension figures in this in a later chapter).

I find that fascinating. I also think it is exactly right, and why the New Testament refers to the healings of Jesus not just as "miracles" but also as "signs." Miracles wow us, but signs say something to us. They point somewhere. They refer to something beyond themselves. That is, signs *preach*—about who God is and what he does. They testify to what God is *always* and *finally* doing among us in Christ. C. S. Lewis remarked that the miracles of Jesus are instances where "the incarnate God does suddenly and locally something that God has done or will do in general." The feeding of the multitudes, for example, is but a "compressed" example of how God is *always* feeding humanity with bread from the earth. "Each miracle writes for us in small letters something that God has already written, or will write, in letters almost too large to be noticed, across the whole canvas of Nature," Lewis says. "They do close and small and, as it were, in focus what God at other times does so large that men do not attend to it."[2]

Or as the poet Wendell Berry puts it:

> The miraculous is not extraordinary but the common mode of existence. It is our daily bread. Whoever really has considered the lilies of the field or the birds of the air and pondered the improbability of their existence in this warm world within the cold and empty stellar distances will hardly balk at the turning of water into wine—which was, after all, a very small miracle. We forget the greater and still continuing miracle by which water (with soil and sunlight) is turned into grapes.[3]

We are *bathed* in miracles, from the first moment of our existence to the last. *Everything* is a miracle. The Epiphany of Jesus Christ is a revelation of how the miraculous is not exceptional but is already-always our actual situation.

As a pastor, I want the folks I shepherd to know that the Presence has come to dwell among them *for a purpose*. That in ways they cannot fully see or understand, God is working to make their lives and the world around them *right*. That here and there, they will see it with their own eyes; and that even when they don't, they can trust that all God's plans are good because the Scripture teaches that God is determined to do us good all the days of our lives until his right-making purposes in the world are fully accomplished, and that *anytime anything anywhere* in the world goes right, it is evidence that the prayer Jesus taught us to pray is coming to pass: "Thy kingdom come, thy will be done, *on earth as it is in heaven.*"

That is, that *Epiphany* is happening.

CASTING OUT DEMONS

But what of the rest of Matthew's description of the epiphanic presence of Jesus, especially of that feature most curious to modern ears: the deliverance of the demon-possessed?

If we are honest, most of us feel discomfort here. Teaching—great. Healing—maybe a little uncomfortable, but okay. But demons and devils? C'mon. Many regard the whole notion of personal, embodied darkness as silly, even primitive. But there it is in the Scriptures and in the ancient church's testimony, impossible to ignore.

Robert Jenson remarks that it is simply not possible to "do Christian theology without explicit systematic reference to Satan; without systematic use of the concept of evil as person." He goes on:

> Somewhere in being, somewhere out there and in there and down there, there is a subjectivity that comprehensively *despises* the world, that *hates* all things. And that subjectivity, that hatred, that despising, is also antecedent to *our* hatred and despisings.

The devil, for Jenson, is the Hatred behind our hatred; the great Despising behind all our despising; the one who "not only impedes and derails" the goodness of the world "but mocks it." Someone, he wrote, "is having malicious fun with God's creation."[4]

It is to the mockery of the evil one that so much of Jesus' ministry is addressed. The Gospel writers depict the ministry of Jesus as an all-out assault on the reign of hell, marked not only by a proliferation of healings but also by demonic deliverance. Jesus came, in his own words, to bind the strong man (Mark 3:27), to cast the ruler of this world out (John 12:31); John writes that Christ came quite simply "to destroy the devil's work" (1 John 3:8). The great short story writer Flannery O'Connor observed, "My subject in fiction is the action of grace in territory largely held by the devil."[5] That's the Gospels' subject matter, too. The embodied Light dispels embodied darkness. And until we come to grips with that, we won't see the world as clearly as we ought.

I once sat with a man in his late thirties tangled up in a years-long pornography addiction. His wife had caught him—again—and demanded he get help. He came to see me.

The meeting had an air of the perfunctory from the outset. He didn't want to be there. At all. We both knew it. I asked him to tell me the story. And so he began. The addiction started when he was a teenager. In his twenties he reached out for help and got himself into an accountability group. It didn't really work, so . . .

. . . and that was the story. The end. No cycle of struggle and failure and resolve to do better. No fight. Nothing. The man had, for all I could tell, thrown in the towel barely a moment after the bell had rung.

This was so startling as to be positively alarming. And I *was* alarmed. So I challenged him. "I'm confused," I said. "You are about to lose your wife and family over this addiction. And you don't seem to care . . ."

I lingered a moment to see if he'd respond. Seconds passed, slowly. "*Do you care?*" I finally asked.

We had struggled for eye contact throughout. With that challenge, however, we finally established it—and it sent a chill down my spine. Passive as his general demeanor had been, his eyes now glared at me with the unmistakable fire of cold contempt. And I knew: he not only *wanted* the addiction; he despised anyone who dared place a question mark over it.

And that, friends, is demonic. Willed evil is demonic. It overthrows the human personality and thwarts human life. It is the essence of hell, the "perverse and petrified choice" as Dorothy Sayers describes it, "grotesque and ghastly" where "the ruin is . . . complete."[6]

We—all of us—have seen this look elsewhere. It is not the look of the trapped person—broken and contrite and desperate for freedom—but the look of those who have made a kind of tryst with evil. You've seen it in the cold, dead eyes of terrorist mug photos, but also—perhaps closer to your own situation, if you, like me, live in a very divided country—in the angry, glaring eyes of those ready to go to blows with others over political differences. And those are just the tip of the iceberg. Evil is everywhere.

Part of what is so vexing about evil is that it is not rational or explainable, and it will not be reasoned with. In fact, it is almost a mark of its existence that it makes no sense—which is why the church has often spoken of the *mysterium iniquitatis*—the "mystery of iniquity" that resists explanation and argument. Sayers calls it "the thing at the bottom: the idiot and slobbering horror."[7] Which is why you can't really *talk* with evil—it just spouts a never-ending stream of nonsense. Clinical psychiatrist and social commentator M. Scott Peck writes that "one of the characteristics of evil is its desire to confuse"[8]—small wonder, given that Jesus described the devil as "a liar and the father of lies" (John 8:44), who lies with a single aim: to plunder God's good world, to rob us of life.

Is there a cure? Yes. John of Patmos writes:

Then I heard a loud voice in heaven say:
> "Now have come the salvation and the power
>> and the kingdom of our God,
>> and the authority of his Messiah.
> For the accuser of our brothers and sisters,
>> who accuses them before our God day and night,
>> has been hurled down.
> They triumphed over him
>> by the blood of the Lamb
>> and by the word of their testimony;
> they did not love their lives so much
>> as to shrink from death." (Revelation 12:10–11)

"*They* triumphed," says John. The church, in which the Epiphanic Word dwells, the church which is the Body of the Word made flesh spread out across space and time, will finally gain the victory over darkness.

As I write this, it is February. Black History Month. I am deeply grateful for this annual, national rhythm. In a society like ours, still struggling with the demons of our past, we need it.

I didn't grow up with much of an awareness of Martin Luther King Jr. and the civil rights movement. The working- and middle-class central Wisconsin town I was raised in was predominantly white. Our country's history of slavery and racism and the long march toward justice embodied in the civil rights struggle just wasn't part of my world—or if it was, I didn't notice. It was certainly nowhere close to the center of my church's spirituality. Peripheral, at best. A marginal concern.

My study of the prophets of Israel in seminary convinced me that God, however, is concerned—deeply concerned—about structural evil, about the way in which sin insinuates itself not just into human hearts, but into the bones and marrow of a society, sickening and finally killing it. That justice is what happens when Jesus, the Healer, says not just to bedridden people but to bedridden *communities*, "Rise up and walk."

I began thinking about our own society. About our many infractions against the love of God. About *my* infractions, *my* blind spots. And that led me to King and the great struggle against the demon-foe of racism.

When I first encountered King's writings, his words struck me with incredible force. The poetry. The power. The gravitas. They burned with white-hot, scorching light, exposing our society's ills even at a half-century's remove. I couldn't get enough.

I still can't. Every year on Martin Luther King Jr. Day I read his *Letter from a Birmingham Jail*. It's a pilgrimage of sorts for me. A matter of prayer and examination that I think is crucial for my spiritual health. *Search me, O God*, I pray. And every February I make it something of a spiritual discipline to keep King's words close to my heart and, as often as I can, on my lips. I have quoted his sermon *Loving Your Enemies* more times than I can count. "Returning hate for hate," said King, "multiplies hate, adding deeper darkness to a night already devoid of stars. Darkness cannot drive out darkness; only light can do that. Hate cannot drive out hate; only love can do that."[9]

Luminous, *epiphanic* words, those. And not just those but all the words he wrote. In their unflinching confrontation with evil, they burned, and burn still. They burn and they heal.

But let it be noticed: *there is a reason they carry such power.* King's words didn't leap up out of the void. They came from somewhere—from his long upbringing in the Black church, which knew (and still knows) much about oppression and struggle and the promise and power of God to bring freedom to captives. King knew this not only because of his firsthand experience of injustice but also—and crucially—because he knew the scriptures of a once-oppressed people finally and fully embodied in the One who was crucified a slave and raised a king.

The thunderous words of Dr. King grew up out of *that* soil. And while I am grateful, truly grateful, that a secular society like ours fights to cherish and embody his legacy, it is, I think, too easy to forget that at the most fundamental level, the words of the great civil rights champion and the story of Jesus are impossible to disentangle. There is not a speech or sermon of King's that is not soaked to the bone with the words of the Word made flesh. And thus they shook and still shake our society.

> This is what the LORD Almighty says: "In a little while I will once more shake the heavens and the earth, the sea and the dry land. I will shake all nations, and what is desired by all nations will come, and I will fill this house with glory," says the LORD Almighty. (Haggai 2:6–7)

Jesus is God's Shaking-in-Flesh. Epiphany tells us that Jesus has not come to confirm the status quo. He has come to upset it, to disrupt it, to rattle its cages until the locks break. He has come to shatter the hold of darkness on our lives and to set the captives free. "The Savior's teaching is increasing everywhere!" exclaims Saint Athanasius.

> Now that the Divine epiphany has come, the darkness of idols prevails no more. . . . *Since the Word of God has been manifested in a body, and has made known to us His*

own Father, the fraud of the demons is stopped and made to disappear; and men, turning their eyes to the true God, Word of the Father, forsake the idols and come to know the true God.[10]

So it is.
So may it continue to be.

Chapter 3

QUESTIONS FOR DISCUSSION

1. How does the great light of Epiphany strengthen your understanding of the story of Jesus?

2. Which part of this chapter most resonated with you? Most challenged you?

3. Where else do you see the presence of evil at work in our society? What might a Christian response to it look like?

4

LENT

The Weakness of Power,
the Power of Weakness

For the foolishness of God is wiser than human wisdom,
and the weakness of God is stronger than human strength.
—1 CORINTHIANS 1:25

To put aside power is Godlike.
—MARILYNNE ROBINSON, *Reading Genesis*

I have this experience often as a preacher:
I pray and study for a message. I am confident in what I've prepared; I can feel it burning in my bones.

Sunday comes. I preach and preach well.

I know this—or at least I think I do—because people are visibly moved while I'm delivering the sermon. I can see it on their faces. The moment that R. S. Thomas spoke of—the preacher catching fire and burning with strange light—thank God, *thank God*, is happening. I'm on fire and I can feel it. Laughter and tears and amens in abundance.

I conclude. We rise to pray and confess our sins. I call them to the Table.

They stream forward. We eat the sacred meal, sing the doxology and receive the familiar words of benediction with glad hearts, Moses's blessing falling like rain on dry land: *May the Lord bless you and keep you; may he cause his face to shine upon you and be gracious to you; may the Lord turn his face toward you and grant you his peace. In the name of the Father, and of the Son, and of the Holy Spirit, amen . . .* They bask in the warmth of those good, old, reassuring words.

The church empties. Some stay behind to kindly pay me a compliment or two. *That was the best message I've ever heard, Pastor*, they'll sometimes say, and *My heart was so stirred by your words*, and *I'm so grateful to sit under your preaching ministry*, and so forth.

I receive their encouragements with gratitude, always. The work is hard and sometimes lonely and it's nice to feel seen and appreciated. Their kind remarks feel good and nourish me. I drive home with a deep sense of satisfaction . . .

. . . which lasts until Monday, when I discover yet again that—the power of yesterday's message notwithstanding— people's lives are still a disordered mess, our social and political alliances are still dubious at best, and that despite my efforts, too many of my congregants are still operating within a guiding belief system that is dreadfully sub-biblical, even heretical.

Have they heard nothing I've said?

I am forced, in other words, to face the fact that my words, for all their beauty and power, for whatever "strange and gracious" light they demonstrated, have ultimately failed. Or so it seems to me.

Which makes me wonder, is failure—not just the failure of preaching, but of any human action designed to motivate change—a *flaw* or a *feature* of the system? And what might that mean for how we think about our lives, our world?

On to Lent . . .

MIRACLE, MYSTERY, AND AUTHORITY

Lent is the forty-day period of spiritual preparation for Easter that begins on Ash Wednesday and concludes with Palm Sunday. It's a time of struggle with what Christians have traditionally called "the world, the flesh, and the devil"—demons within and without. A time also to remember that the struggle—however difficult—is not in vain, because Jesus has entered the struggle with us and emerged victorious.

Appropriately, the first Sunday of Lent focuses on the temptation of Christ, when the Word made flesh, still dripping from his baptism, is led by the Holy Spirit into the wilderness, where he squares off with the evil one. Forty days of fasting to match the forty years of Israel's wanderings in their own wilderness. Jesus, hungry and tired from his fast, is now sorely tried.

The temptations are familiar to many of us. Each deliberately echoes Israel's history, recalls Israel's failures: the failure to trust God for provision; the failure to trust God for security; the temptation to put God to the test and "prove"—on our terms—that he is faithful. Israel's failures are our failures, too.[1] And Jesus, the true Israelite, the true Human, stands in for God's people, for us. The temptation narratives are given that we might know that Jesus, the Faithful One, succeeds where we fail; indeed, that we may know that by his success, we too will not finally fail.

I heard many sermons about the temptations of Jesus when I was young. *Temptations will come*, we were told. *The enemy is out to get you like he was out to get Jesus. And like Jesus, you can overcome him by knowing your Bible.*

Well-intended, those sermons. They weren't wrong. I see now, however, that they also weren't *right enough*. The testing of Jesus in the wilderness is not first or primarily about us. It's about him. Jesus will be faithful where Israel was not; his obedience will overcome the fall of Adam's race, *our* fall. That's what makes it good news, what makes it *gospel*.

So far so good. But there's more. What is not remarked upon nearly enough is *what is actually at stake in the temptations themselves for Jesus*. Dostoevsky's Grand Inquisitor in *The Brothers Karamazov* gets it right when he argues that the three temptations were (and are) precisely this: ways of exercising power over a violent and rebellious humanity. "There are three powers, three powers alone, able to conquer and hold captive forever the conscience of these impotent rebels for their happiness," cries the Inquisitor: "those forces are miracle, mystery, and authority."[2]

Prove that you can provide bread, says the evil one, and the masses will pledge their allegiance to you. Garb yourself in the mystique of the supernatural, and the fascination of the crowds will be yours. Seize the reins of absolute authority, and the nations will fall down in worship at your feet.

The temptations, in other words, are ways of coercing humanity's allegiance.

And Jesus flatly refuses them.

What does that say about him? About God? About us?

THE STRANGE REIGN OF GOD

"God reigns over the nations," says the psalmist. "God sits on his holy throne" (Psalm 47:8 ESV)—an affirmation repeated throughout the Scriptures, the announcement pealing like thunder across the biblical canon and landing with a dramatic clap in Revelation. At the end of history, the multitudes worship God, saying:

Hallelujah!
For the Lord our God
    the Almighty reigns.
Let us rejoice and exult
    and give him the glory! (Revelation 19:6–7 ESV)

And as the text is read and prayed, pondered and preached, our own hearts burn with adoration. "The LORD reigns; let the earth rejoice!" (Psalm 97:1 ESV) is our eager and earnest cry. God, our God, is in charge. God reigns. And this is good news.

But perhaps, I wonder, are we just *a little too eager*, for it seems to me that if we really want to say "God reigns," we'll have to be taught by the Spirit what that means—and it will be a long and often bewildering instruction.

There is a strangeness to the way the God of the Bible, the God of Jesus Christ, reigns. It is not, of course, anything particularly odd for a religion to assert that God or the gods are sovereign and powerful and very much in charge. "God reigns" is stock-in-trade religious language. Of what use is an impotent deity?

But then we start reading our text and are surprised to discover *just how* the God revealed in Jesus chooses to exercise sovereignty.

He *could have* prevented our first parents from eating the forbidden fruit . . .

But he didn't.

He *could have* prevented Israel from the disaster of the calf-idol . . .

But he didn't.

He *could have* prevented David's great and dark moral collapse . . .

But he didn't.

The examples could be multiplied. "God reigns," we say, and say rightly. And that reign, when you read the text of Scripture, is strange. Very strange. The content that fills the affirmation baffles as much as—and perhaps more than—it comforts.

It becomes even more baffling when you read of the times when God *does* exercise power in direct and obvious ways—behaving, in other words, like a sovereign monarch might—the archetypical example being the flood, where God declares his intent to judge the world with a dramatic demonstration of power and to start humanity afresh.

Well and good, we think. And God does what he says. But no sooner have the floodwaters of divine judgment receded than we read of Noah's drunken debauchery and Ham's degrading behavior toward his father. Doom moves over our hearts like an encroaching winter storm. *It didn't work*, we think. *And if that didn't work, will anything?*

The failures multiply. Egypt, despite the plagues, continues its wickedness. Israel, despite repeated judgments, continues its rebellion. The nations, prophetic warnings and divine calamities notwithstanding, continue their wicked ways, and the promise of the Psalter that "the nobles of the nations [will] assemble as the people of the God of Abraham, for the kings of the earth belong to God; he is greatly exalted" (Psalm 47:9) hangs suspended in midair, looking less likely with each turn of the page.

Theologian Chris Green puts bluntly what we struggle (and perhaps even think blasphemous) to admit: *none* of the judgments of the Old Testament actually *worked*.[3] The hope that direct power will bring about the kingdom appears, with the close of the Old Testament, to be one long, abject failure in the same direction.

DODGING POWER

Naturally, then, we meet Jesus in the pages of the Gospels and find ourselves thinking with the crowds that now, at last, things will be different. Jesus has power, real power, and he knows how to use it. The season of Epiphany gestures in precisely this direction. Miracle, mystery, and authority are everywhere. Unsurprisingly, the crowds flock to him, hanging on his every word. "What is this? A new teaching—and with authority!" (Mark 1:27). The fascination of the multitudes is all his. The anticipation of revolution is in the air. He needs only to take it, to capitalize on it, to claim his rightful place. As in the wilderness, so here: power is laid at his feet.

And just like in the wilderness, he walks away from it.

Not once, but *every* time. In the gospel of John, the ducking and dodging of power is serial. Jesus doesn't take public credit for the miracle in Cana (John 2:9). He slips away into the crowd after healing the man at the pool of Bethesda (5:13). He quite literally runs for the hills when the recently fed masses at the Sea of Galilee try to make him "king by force" (6:15).

In the other three gospels, the pattern is the same. When in the early days of his ministry the hysteria around his growing popularity reaches a fever pitch, he declares that it is time to preach elsewhere and then gets up and leaves, *just like that* (Mark 1:38). When the disciples ask if they should call down the fires of divine judgment like Elijah did upon those who didn't welcome him, Jesus rebukes them (Luke 9:55). And when he is about to be arrested and led away under guard, he declares explicitly: "Do you think I cannot call on my Father, and he will at once put at my disposal more than twelve legions of angels? But how then would the Scriptures be fulfilled that say it must happen in this way?" (Matthew 26:53–54).

King Jesus—the reign of God in person—categorically throws off power and ends his life quivering on a cross with humanity still an abominable mess.

The Bible is a strange book indeed.

ABSOLUTELY NOTHING

A family in the church came to see me. They were at loggerheads with their teenage son. He was tangled up in the wrong crowd at school, and his behavior had slowly deteriorated, reaching a breaking point when he was pulled over for speeding and subsequently taken into custody for marijuana possession after the police officer smelled pot in the car and then discovered a couple of joints in the console.

The arrest sent his parents over the edge. After bailing him out and bringing him home, an angry confrontation ensued. Seething with confused rage, the parents pressured the boy to explain what was going on, to answer for himself. But he would not. He just stood there, stone-faced and sullen.

As the confrontation continued, the parents watched the windows of the boy's soul begin to shutter and seal. Undeterred, they ratcheted up the pressure and raised the stakes, punishing and threatening more severe punishments if their son didn't right himself.

He kept closing down. After a long and wearisome night, they sent him to his room and retreated to theirs, defeated. They slept and woke in the morning and promptly went to their son's room to apologize for how dramatically they had overreacted the night before.

The apology fell on deaf ears.

Weeks and then months passed. While there were no further dramatic incidents, it was clear to them that their son's heart had withdrawn into some place they could not reach. He was rarely home, and despite their pleas, he stopped coming with them to church. When he did make an occasional appearance around the house—mostly for food—greetings went generally unanswered, questions received one-word replies, and eye contact was sedulously avoided. The worst fears of the couple were being realized: they were losing their son.

And so they had reached out to me.

"What do we do?" they asked when we sat down. "What *can* we do?"

I knew what they were looking for: a foolproof way to get their boy back. And how badly I wanted to give their worried hearts exactly what they desired: a time-honored, airtight strategy; a money-back-guaranteed method for rescuing wayward kids.

How badly I wanted that for them.

This kind of thing, by the way, is par for the course for pastors. Eugene Peterson says that folks often expect either miracles or answers from their pastors, who "are in the awkward position of refusing"—or, I would add, being unable!—"to give what a great many people assume it is our assigned job to give. We are in the embarrassing position of disappointing people in what they think they have a perfect right to get from us."[4]

As I sat there with this couple's question lingering in the air, I thought of a remark made by John Ames, the central character in Marilynne Robinson's novel *Gilead*. Ames, who is both a pastor and a father, is nearing the end of his life, and preaches a sermon on Hagar and Ishmael and the binding, or sacrifice, of Isaac in Genesis 21–22. It is not easy (this sermon never is). And Ames concludes that all parents "must finally give [their] child up to the wilderness and trust to the providence of God." He goes on, saying, "Great faith is required to give the child up, trusting God to honor the parents' love for him by assuring that there will indeed be angels in the wilderness."[5]

Stress over the future of our children and feelings of help-lessness over being out of control is apparently nothing new for the people of God, I thought. *Which may or may not be a comfort to these dear people. But either way, it is true, and it needs to be said . . .*

Taking a deep breath and looking them dead in the eye, I answered, "Nothing"—and then watched the last dregs of hope drain from their souls. "There is absolutely nothing you can do," I said, "except maybe this—give your son to Jesus; and keep the porch light on for him."

THE WEAKNESS OF POWER

Relationship is a deep mystery. Maybe the deepest. You can spend a lifetime searching out its subtleties and feel you know less at the end of your quest than you did at the start. But one thing about relationship is certain, and it is this:

Direct power is perfectly useless on it.

Which sheds light on what is happening in Jesus' refusal to leverage power to bring about the kingdom. He simply will not save the world in that way. But why?

The priest Robert Farrar Capon has written at length on this theme.[6] "If God wants to turn this messed-up world into a city or a kingdom," Capon asks, "why doesn't he just knock some heads together, put all the baddies under a large, flat rock, and get on with the job?"[7]

Of course, God *does* do this, according to Capon, at least once—at the flood, as we've already seen—but even there, "when the final, scriptural point of the episode is made," it reveals an entirely different notion of power:

God says he is never going to do anything like that again. He says that his answer to the evil that keeps the world from becoming the city of God will not, paradoxically, involve direct intervention on behalf of the city. Instead, he makes a covenant of nonintervention with the world; he sets his bow in the cloud—the symbolic development of which could either be that he hangs all his effective weapons against wickedness up on the wall or, more bizarrely still, that he points them skyward, at himself instead of us.[8]

Marilynne Robinson concurs. While the flood story might be taken as an affirmation of the divine use of direct power, when the tale finally concludes, God "repented of the destruction He had caused, and even though, being God, He could have remade the world so that evil and violence were excluded from it, He forgave, or forbore, the corrupt thoughts of human hearts. . . . He chose to let us be, to let time yield what it will—within the vast latitude granted by providence."[9] God's penchant for doing just that across the book of Genesis leads Robinson to this conclusion: "To put aside power is Godlike."[10]

Not, of course, that direct interventions are automatically evil. If a criminal is loose in my neighborhood, I am rightly grateful for the presence of the police to restrain them. Direct power can have an appropriate place in a world constantly threatened by chaos. It's not a bad thing, necessarily.

Unfortunately, writes Capon, it "has a whopping limitation. If you take the view that one of the chief objects in life is to remain in loving relationships with other people, straight-line power"—that is, the use of force to get results—"becomes useless."[11] For example, if a relationship with a teenage son becomes fraught, "at some very early crux in that difficult, personal relationship, the whole thing will be destroyed unless you—who, on any reasonable view, should be allowed to use straight-line power—simply refuse to use it; unless, in other words, you decide that instead of dishing out justifiable pain and punishment, you are willing, quite foolishly, to take a beating yourself."[12]

In fact, as Capon spies it, the ministry of Jesus itself embodies the shift from direct, "straight-line" power to something more paradoxical—a shift seen in the movement from Epiphany to Lent. Whereas in Epiphany we see Jesus as a "plausible, intervening, advice-giving, miracle-working Messiah," as the Passion begins to loom on the horizon, Jesus becomes "a dying, rising, and disappearing one."[13]

Jesus, we might say, *is the God-in-flesh who came among us and took a beating at our hands so that we might be reconciled to the Father who forever keeps the porch light on for us.*

The strategy may seem ridiculous. It may seem weak. It may seem ineffective. But—if the gospel is to be believed at all—it is by such things that the world is won. As Paul wrote to the Corinthians:

> The message of the cross is foolishness to those who are perishing, but to us who are being saved it is the power of God. . . . For the foolishness of God is wiser than human wisdom, and the weakness of God is stronger than human strength. (1 Corinthians 1:18, 25)

In the Passion of his Christ, God hangs the bow in the clouds. And so we are saved.

IMPOSING NOTHING

It's the kindness of God that leads the world to repentance (Romans 2:4). The *kindness*; not the power. "On her part,"

Pope John Paul II once wrote, speaking of the church's mission in the world, "the Church addresses people with full respect for their freedom. Her mission does not restrict freedom but rather promotes it. *The Church proposes; she imposes nothing.*"[14]

The church *proposes*. Never *imposes*. Like a lover appealing to the beloved: "Will you . . . ?" The ball is in the beloved's court. Power is useless. It is on the beloved to freely consent—or not. And the lover will not have it any other way. A coerced yes is no yes at all.

But—and to get this is to grasp the nettle of this whole issue—*the lover can do nothing to bring the yes about.* By definition, then, the lover is weak, and will quite possibly look foolish, even very foolish. But that's the gambit. It's the only way it works.

I asked earlier, why won't Jesus save the world with brute force? The answer by now should be clear: because he can't.[15] Because if relationship and not mere servitude is what God is after, then power just won't do the trick. Only patient love—which respects the freedom of the other, which is therefore fundamentally "weak"—will do. Catherine LaCugna explains, "Community exists for the sake of friendship and presupposes relationships built on love. Friendship results from persons who are free, who do not relate out of fear of the other or fear for self."[16]

No one was ever bullied into genuine relationship. Not with others. Not with God. "Merely to override a human will," said C. S. Lewis, "would be for Him useless. He cannot ravish. He can only woo."[17] Or as Dostoyevsky's Ivan Karamazov says of Jesus, "He moves silently in their midst with a gentle smile of infinite compassion," which "stirs their hearts with responsive love"[18]—a love that utterly confounds the Grand Inquisitor.

Part of our call in the world, therefore, is to embody precisely this kind of love, this way of being, in the way that we relate to others. "Dear friends, since God so loved us, we also ought to love one another," writes John, for "in this world we are like Jesus" (1 John 4:11, 17). Taken up by our baptism into Christ, his way of being is "mirrored in our relations with others as we live a life of service to God."[19]

Or at least it is *supposed* to be. For we are slow to believe these things. Painfully slow. And our witness, our *world*, suffers just to the extent that we refuse to put our full confidence in the strange way that God reigns.

Among evangelicals, for example—a tribe of which I count myself part—historian Kristin Kobes Du Mez has provided a sobering study of how the political chaos of the last few years is at least partly the result of evangelicals' "embrace of militant masculinity, an ideology that enshrines patriarchal authority and condones the callous display of power, at home and abroad."[20] In a similar vein, author Katelyn Beaty has shown how celebrity, which she defines as "social power without proximity," is itself not just a bug but a *feature* of evangelical Christianity in the United States. Evangelicals, Beaty contends, see high-profile, celebrity leadership (*power-full* leadership, that is) as critical to the advance of the gospel—which means that we're willing to bend our structures (and sometimes even the rules) to "platform" people. And, of course, we'll do the same to protect their platform at all costs once they have it (since our own power suddenly depends on it).[21] The system is perverse.

Those examples are just the tip of the iceberg—and not at all confined to my tribe, for every group has its own foibles. The point is that whenever we substitute power for love, we show that we are far less like Jesus and more like the Grand

Inquisitor in Ivan Karamazov's fable—the Inquisitor who looks back across history with its wars and revolutions and tragedies and regards the decision of Jesus to reject power as an abject failure, idiotic to the core, finally declaring, "I awakened and would not serve [your] madness. I turned back and joined the ranks of those *who have corrected thy work*."[22]

What a statement—and one of which we, too, are guilty: trying to correct the "failure" of God. The epidemic of moral bankruptcy among church leaders and the spiritual shallowness of much of the Western church should come as no surprise to us. We have been too long enamored with power. Decades ago, Henri Nouwen observed that "one of the greatest ironies in the history of Christianity is that its leaders constantly gave in to the temptation of power"—though the object of our worship and devotion is the Jesus "who did not cling to his divine power but emptied himself and became as we are." The greatest temptation we face is the temptation to think that power is a way to proclaim the gospel. Indeed, "every time we see a major crisis in the history of the church," Nouwen observed, "a major cause of rupture is the power exercised by those who claim to be followers of the poor and powerless Jesus.[23]

THE POWER OF LOVE
What does it look like when God shows up in our midst to manifest the reign of righteousness? Brute strength? Raw power? A dramatic overthrow of the Resistance? Surely that is what we might have expected, unconverted as we are.

But Lent tells a different tale—the tale of the one who refused power at every turn, who rides into Jerusalem humble and lowly, who stoops to wash the feet of his disciples like a common servant before finally dying a victim's death—the foolish end to a foolish life that somehow manifests the kingdom, winning fools like us to the wisdom and love of God. St. Irenaeus—one of the earliest and most insightful fathers of the early church—hits the nail on the head: "The words 'the government is upon His shoulder' figuratively signify the Cross, to which his arms were nailed . . . it is the Cross which He calls His government, the sign of His kingship."[24]

So now to return to the question we've been wrestling with: *Is failure a flaw or a feature of the system?*

I have come to see that it is a feature—and a saving one at that. It is on God, working mysteriously via the "left-handed" ways and means of the Spirit, to awaken hearts to the love made manifest in the One who died in weakness and folly.

On the cross, God kept, and keeps, the porch light on for us.

Christians—from preachers to those in the pews—have a single task and responsibility: testifying to and embodying the cross-shaped love of God wherever they go, doing so in weakness and often folly. Which is precisely what Paul says in 1 Corinthians. The Messiah was made to look like a fool. And we are fools for him and with him. God's fools. And the Spirit is somehow using all that to save the world.

Weakness, friend, is part of the deal. It's a feature of the system. The miracle, whole and entire, lies on God's side, not ours. It always does. To use a sacramental analogy here: the bread and cup of communion do not become more miraculous the more effort we put into making them spectacular. Rosemary and garlic focaccia bread and a fine Beaujolais are not more apt instruments to serve as a channel for the divine life than plain wafers and stale wine. In fact, they may distract from the main point, which is, after all . . . *God*. "We have this treasure in jars of clay to show that this all-surpassing power is from God and not from us," said Paul (2 Corinthians 4:7).

"God never overpowers," says Ronald Rolheiser. "God's power in this world is never the power of a muscle, a speed, a physical attractiveness, a brilliance, or a grace which (as the contemporary expression has it) blows you away and makes you shout, 'Yes! Yes! There is a God!'" While this is, more or less, the way the world thinks about power, God's power "is more muted, more helpless, more shamed, and more marginalized. But it lies at a deeper level, at the ultimate base of things, and will, in the end, gently have the final say."[25]

God's paradoxical power is the power of love, and it will—rest assured—have the final say, for it is precisely by the long, circuitous route of salvation history, embodied in the strange sojourn of Jesus to the cross, that the truth finally wins the world over, as every knee bows and every tongue finally confesses that the holy fool hanging powerless on a tree outside Jerusalem is nothing less than the reign of God in person.

Chapter 4

QUESTIONS FOR DISCUSSION

1. What did you make of this chapter's distinction between different kinds of power? Where have you seen that distinction at work?

2. Has there been a time in your life when "weakness" proved to be the better strategy?

3. Where do you see the temptation to power spoiling the church's witness?

GOOD FRIDAY

Safe with Jesus

My God, my God, why have you forsaken me?
—**MATTHEW 27:46**

There is no pit so deep that He is not deeper still.
—**BETSIE TEN BOOM**, quoted in Corrie Ten Boom, *The Hiding Place*

Lent ends on a chipper note—the jubilant welcome of Jesus into Jerusalem on the day known as Palm Sunday and commemorated by Christians around the world. Yet for all its jubilation, a storm is gathering. Like Jesus himself, the reader familiar with the story knows that the joy of Palm Sunday will end in an unmitigated disaster: the death of the Son of God by crucifixion.[1]

I have already mentioned my appreciation for the church of my youth—a tambourine-toting, flag-waving, tongue-talking charismatic congregation. I am and forever will be grateful for the gifts it gave me—not least a deep and abiding sense that to love and worship God is to know Deity as everywhere-always present, ready to break through, able to save.

As a pastor, as a *Christian*, I believe these things. As I've said, I believe that it is right to contend for incursions of the divine life—for the marriage to be restored, for the disaster to be averted, for the body to be raised. I have been witness to many such stories. I thank God for them. "You turned my wailing into dancing" (Psalm 30:11).

And yet, I have also been witness to many others (maybe more) that did not end on a triumphant note. The marriage wasn't restored. The disaster wasn't averted. The body wasn't raised. What do you do with such stories?

My childhood church—along with, frankly, the entire charismatic movement—tended to struggle with them. When the desired outcome slipped through our fingers, we wondered whose faith had failed, or worse, whether Deity had faltered. A heavy load of condemnation and a shattered image of God were the price we paid for a one-sided and triumphalist understanding of the Christian faith.

We thought of ourselves as *Easter* Christians, after all, and while we (somewhat reluctantly) celebrated Good Friday, the death of Jesus had little or nothing to do with our actual, lived spirituality. At best the cross was prelude, certainly not "the truth about everything"; it would have never occurred to us to think of it as "the spiritual architecture of Christian experience,"[2] as theologian Richard John Neuhaus put it. At worst, the cross was a cumbersome distraction to the victorious life. Theologian Dietrich Bonhoeffer's claim that "only a suffering God can help"[3] would have been unintelligible to us.

And we were the poorer for it, as we all are when we fail to reckon with the disaster that took place on that good and terrible day.

DEATH-DENIAL

Much as we would like, the story of God will not permit us to anxiously skip by the horror of Golgotha. Paul insisted that the death of Christ was the foundation of the early church's preaching, the very heartbeat of its message. To the Corinthians, he wrote:

> For what I received I passed on to you as of first importance: that Christ died for our sins according to the Scriptures, that he was buried, that he was raised on the third day according to the Scriptures. (1 Corinthians 15:3–4)

"He was raised!" we want to shout—racing past the cross to the empty tomb, anxious not only to avoid the reality of death but also, if possible, to turn back the clock, returning life to a form we can recognize—which is what the empty tomb surely signifies to many of us. Easter is our collective sigh of relief that finally, after all, life will go on just as before.

But death is real. And life cannot, will not, go on as before. It is the dead man, Jesus, who now lives. His resurrection (and ours) is not a resuscitation, not a return. It is something else entirely.

We ignore these truths to our detriment.

Some years ago, a well-known and influential pastor from my theological tribe was diagnosed with cancer. These things happen. Hard? Yes. Unusual? No. We have it on good authority: "In this world you will have trouble" (John 16:33).

What especially complicated the situation was the fact that a great deal of this pastor's popularity came from his reputation as a faith-healer. A cancer diagnosis, therefore, was not just hard; it was theologically and practically unthinkable—an assault on a worldview, a ministry.

The pastor and his family went into denial. The church was not told—and why would they need to be since, as they believed, divine healing was not only assured; it was also *already accomplished* by the finished work of Christ? And therefore, life and ministry could and did go on largely as before—full schedules and lots of travel to far-off places to tell people the good news of, among other things, God's will to heal. Nothing to be alarmed of here.

Not until the eleventh hour, when it became impossible to ignore, was the news made public. When, for the cancer's ravaging of his body, the pastor could no longer preach, then and only then was the congregation informed—with the sparsest of details. The seriousness of the pastor's health crisis was constantly downplayed. No talk of succession or contingency plans. No space for people to absorb the impact of the devastating news and grieve. Just gauzy, vague reports and glib affirmations that no one, *really*, had anything to be concerned about.

One is tempted to call it a pathological commitment to the status quo.

Within weeks the pastor was dead, the congregation left in a deeply uncertain lurch. Perhaps worse, because the family was so fully convinced that healing was on the way, no one ever really said goodbye. Indeed, in the hours after he died, the family kept vigil over him in confident prayer, fully (self-) assured that the Lord would raise him up.

Need I say? He was not raised.

You may scoff at that story, but the truth is that denial in order to maintain the status quo is closer to all of us than we realize—and just as deadly. I am thinking of the aging pastor who in denial of his waning strength stays at his post too long and permanently hamstrings his congregation. Or of the woman who, clinging ferociously to her dream of a happy family life, remains in an abusive marriage. Or of the too many people I know who, refusing to accept that the country they once knew and loved is changing, violate not only their own values but every norm of decency and civility because of their fear of the future.

Let us put the sharpest point on it that we can: the fear of death robs us of our humanity, thwarts our lives, makes us unwise. In trying to save our lives, we lose them. Which is exactly what Jesus said would happen. "Whoever wants to save their life will lose it" (Matthew 16:25).

ARS MORIENDI

But suppose we didn't fear death. Or at least knew we didn't *need* to fear it. The gospel tells us this is so. So says the writer of Hebrews: "Since the children have flesh and blood, he too shared in their humanity so that by his death he might break the power of him who holds the power of death—that is, the devil—and free those who all their lives were held in slavery by their fear of death" (Hebrews 2:14–15).

It is not *death* that finally enslaves us, but our *fear* of death. "It is the Bent One, the lord of your world, who wastes your lives and befouls them with flying from what you know will overtake you in the end," says Oyarsa, lord of Malacandra, to the hooligans who set out to conquer his planet in the climactic scene of C. S. Lewis's *Out of the Silent Planet*. "If you were subjects of [God] you would have peace."[4]

From the fear of what we know will overtake us, the gospel tells us, we have been freed so that, in a wildly paradoxical twist, our relationship with death is no longer antagonistic but—dare we say?—cordial, even collaborative. By the death of the Son, proud Death has been humbled and made a servant of the saints, their personal concierge into the Life. Isn't that, after all, what our baptism signals—that death is made a portal into life? "Don't you know that all of us who were baptized into Christ Jesus were baptized into his death?

We were therefore buried with him through baptism into death in order that, just as Christ was raised from the dead through the glory of the Father, we too may live a new life" (Romans 6:3–4).

Accordingly, it has been said that Christian discipleship is a long study in the *ars moriendi*—the art of dying well. The fathers and mothers of the desert—the first monastics— understood that the embrace of death was the root of a wise and wholesome life. Amma Sarah said, "I put out my foot to ascend the ladder, and I place death before my eyes before going up it."[5] As Father John O'Donohue notes in his poem "For Death," from the first moment of life, death walks beside us. Recognizing this gives us the ability to decide how to live a good and wholesome life.[6]

Good Friday teaches us to say: Only those who by the cross have abandoned their fear of death can befriend their death and so live a life worthy of the calling. We can do this because our good Jesus abandoned *his* human fear of death and entered it with and as the undiminished presence of God. David spoke better than he knew when he said, "Even though I walk through the valley of the shadow of death, I will fear no evil, *for you are with me*" (Psalm 23:4 ESV, emphasis added).

We can face death without fear.

And even befriend it.

Because Jesus entered it on our behalf.

And in so doing, turned it inside out.

GOD ON A CROSS

I have come to see that no small part of my vocation as a pastor is helping people know Jesus as their forerunner and companion in death, teaching them to rest in that knowledge, so that in quietness of heart they might bed down with Jesus in the grave, where he has gone for us, with us, as one of us. When we can do this, it changes everything.

When as a young pastor I sat next to Laura's bed in that sterile hospital room, holding her hand with tears streaming down both her face and mine, I remember feeling unprepared and helpless in the face of her anxious queries. "Why is this happening? Where is God? Why isn't he doing anything to help me? When is this nightmare going to be over?" Her emaciated body, her tears, the puncture wounds from needles all over her arms—what could I say that would make any difference? My mind thrashed about for anything, *anything*, I could do or say that might ease Laura's burden.

That's when I noticed it: on the opposite wall, another emaciated body hung, weeping, with skin punctured and head bowed. A crucifix.

It suddenly hit me how profoundly symbolic the crucifix is. *Jesus is still on it*—as opposed to the Protestant cross, which is empty. Not, of course, that Catholics believe that Jesus is still dead; but rather, the crucifix reminds us that God entered, *really entered*, our death when Jesus died—*and that Jesus really died*. The crucifixion was not, as some early heretical Christian groups believed, a mirage, a sham, or a clever trick. No, the death of the Son was real; likewise, the resurrection *is the resurrection of the Crucified*—not a reversal; not a return to "the way things were." There never is and never will be a going back. Only a going forward into whatever transformations God has in store for us.

The crucifix captures that for me in a way that an empty cross does not—for an empty cross runs the risk of conveying that Jesus pulled a Houdini on death rather than submitting to it, experiencing its horrors, and thereby robbing it of its power.

That was the pastoral epiphany I needed. "Laura," I said, "look over at the wall. What do you see?"

"A crucifix," she replied, her voice barely a whisper.

"That's right. I think that's your answer. Jesus has made your broken body his, and his yours. He is here, now, closer than either of us can ever fathom. You can trust him."

A sense of Presence stole into the room, thick as a cloud. We both felt it, and we smiled and gave thanks to God through sobs.

If the Christian claims be true, we can and *must* say that the Crucified One is nothing less than God from God, Light from Light, True God from True God, begotten not made, of One Being with the Father, through whom all things were made. It forces us to say that the One who made the world was murdered upon it. That the hands which hung the sun and the stars were pinned to the hard wood of the cross. That the One who—paradox of paradoxes—cannot suffer *did suffer* "for us and for our salvation," as the Nicene Creed declares.

And that just as he hung helpless on that tree, so also all our hope in life and in death hangs on him.

THE ONE WHO CRIES FROM THE CROSS

Theologian Jürgen Moltmann begins his classic work *The Crucified God* by asking, "Who is God in the cross of the Christ who is abandoned by God?"[7] That is, what exactly is happening when the Son cries out to the Father in defiant agony, "My God, my God, why have you forsaken me?" And what is that moment telling us about God?

I first read Moltmann's words right around the time of Laura's crisis. They have become definitional for me, the way I "read" reality. Just who is the God who in the cross of the Christ cries out in dereliction to God?

In his memoir about surviving the Nazi concentration camps, Elie Wiesel describes witnessing the hanging of a young boy. The boy, perhaps thirteen or fourteen, had been suspected of helping stockpile weapons for a prisoners' revolt. The boy was sentenced, along with the other dissidents—grown men—to death by hanging.

As the moment of execution loomed, Wiesel heard someone in the crowd behind him ask, "Where is merciful God? Where is he?" The men and boy were made to stand on chairs and ropes were placed around their necks. The chairs were tipped over. The men died quickly, their heavier bodies hastening their demise. The young boy, much lighter, lingered long—almost a half hour—between life and death, struggling for breath, as the prisoners were forced to look on, their lynching a cautionary tale for other would-be dissidents. Wiesel writes:

> Behind me, I heard the same man asking:
> "For God's sake, where is God?"
> And from within, I heard a voice answer:
> "Where He is? This is where—hanging here from this gallows."[8]

It is not hard to know what Wiesel, an atheist, intends by this story. His memoir details the way in which his Jewish faith struggled to survive the horrors of his experience. The death of the young boy was a watershed for Wiesel (who also was a boy at the time), a moment when his concept of God fell apart, reducing his faith to rubble. Later, he gathers with his Jewish brothers in the hell of the camp for the celebration of Rosh Hashanah, the Jewish new year. "My eyes had opened and I was alone, terribly alone in a world without God, without man. Without love or mercy. I was nothing but ashes now," he writes. "In the midst of these men assembled for prayer, I felt like an observer, a stranger."[9]

The experience for Wiesel was an annihilation—of belief, of his sense of place in the world, of his connection to others.

It is difficult to comprehend the horrors that Weisel and others experienced in the camps. The heart reels and staggers when reading memoirs like Elie Wiesel's *Night*. What hells we create on planet Earth. We are so often tempted to look away.

But Good Friday calls us to look again, to see more than meets the eye. It teaches us to comprehend all things within the double vision made possible by the gospel. In the story of God the Son's sojourn among us, the gospel invites us to see suffering transfigured by the strange and gracious light that is Jesus—*for in Christ, God did hang on the gallows.*

And I believe that means that God was with that boy that day, and with young Elie, too, as he was and is and forever will be with every sufferer in the extremity of all their suffering. Knowing this brings hope. Theologian James Cone describes that hope in *The Cross and the Lynching Tree* when he speaks of how Black Christians found solace in the cross especially during the lynching era. "The spirituals, gospel songs, and hymns focused on how Jesus achieved salvation for the least through his *solidarity* with them even unto death. There were more songs, sermons, prayers, and testimonies about the cross than any other theme. The cross was the foundation on which their faith was built." The cross, writes Cone, "places God in the midst of crucified people, in the midst of people who are hung, shot, burned, and tortured."[10]

When the fourteenth-century English anchoress Julian of Norwich hung between life and death, she looked to the cross and found comfort: "Whilst I looked at the cross I was secure and safe," she writes. And when a voice came to her tempting her to look beyond the cross to heaven, she showed not only her theological wherewithal but her deep, deep love for Jesus, replying, "No, I cannot, for you [the Crucified Jesus] are my heaven . . . and this has always been a comfort to me, that I chose Jesus as my heaven in all times of suffering and of sorrow."[11]

Think of it: *Jesus is our heaven*, even when we find ourselves in the lowest pit—for that is the mission of Immanuel from the cradle to the grave and beyond: God's commitment to be *God-with-us* wherever we go. As the psalmist said, even "if I make my bed in hell, you are there" (Psalm 139:8 GW).

In Christ Jesus that is so. God in our hell. And that is good news.

I realize that talking this way may be challenging. And I think that this is because our theology is not rich enough. Across the Christian tradition, the notion of "hell" is more than a "place"; more even than a way of describing the pain we endure living in broken bodies under the curse of sin and death. It is—much more profoundly—a way of talking about the spiritual and psychological and existential agony of separation from God. John Calvin is helpful here, remarking that "we must not omit the descent to hell" spoken of by the Apostles' Creed, for that descent "was of no little importance to the accomplishment of redemption."[12] For Calvin, Christ's descent into hell is one and the same with Jesus' experience of dereliction on the cross. "No abyss can be imagined more dreadful than to feel that you are abandoned and forsaken of God, and not heard when you invoke him. To such a degree was Christ dejected."[13]

The philosopher G. K. Chesterton observes that Christ's passion contains a "distinct emotional suggestion": "That the author of all things (in some unthinkable way) went through not only agony but doubt"—a doubt seen especially in the cry of dereliction from the cross, "the cry which confessed that God was forsaken of God." There is no other god, says Chesterton, "who has himself been in revolt." Christ is the only divinity to ever utter isolation—in which "God seemed for an instant to be an atheist."[14]

I have often leveraged Chesterton's insight to provide pastoral care for those who have, like Wiesel, told me that they were drowning in a sea of doubt, unsure whether they could believe in God anymore. Mindful that the Second Person also "uttered their isolation," I've found myself saying to them, "You're going to be okay. God is with you and holds you even when you aren't sure you can believe in 'God' anymore." Many times, such counsel visibly puts them at ease. Deconstruction suddenly is transformed from a terrifying void to a kind of bright abyss—or better, an entryway into a new and deeper understanding of God.[15]

I say such things, again, and *can* say such things because Jesus went there. Because he made our human experience—all of it—his. And because the very one who cried out in Godforsakenness *also* finally entrusted himself—and all of us along with him, if indeed he be the representative human—to his Father. In Jesus' final moments, he transformed the human experience of desolation into a prayer of trust when he with his dying breath prayed the prayer of the psalmist, "Father, into your hands I commit my spirit" (Luke 23:46).[16]

Even the human loss of faith has been made part of God, yielded to God, *converted*.

There is literally nowhere we can go from God, because Jesus is our Immanuel.[17]

NOTHING LEFT TO FEAR

It is no part of our task to avoid, explain away, or minimize suffering, in whatever form it comes. Our job, as people of the light, is to tenderly announce the Presence of God to it—in Christ Jesus, God has gone there, is there, will always be there ahead of us, waiting for us. And therefore, the suffering can not only be faced but *embraced*. Full now of the light and life of God-in-flesh, there is nothing left in it to fear.

Jim and Jeannene are a lovely couple in my congregation. They have been married for nearly five decades. They love Jesus and each other and their family and the church, deeply. They are an example of wise and human and holy living.

Two years ago, Jeannene was diagnosed with Parkinson's disease. It is slowly robbing her of strength and vitality. It is also pulling her and Jim's life together out of its longstanding proportion. Parkinson's, as with so many degenerative illnesses, is in its own way a living death—for each day and week and month presents the afflicted and their loved ones with new losses.

I sat with Jim one afternoon at a coffee shop to catch up. He shared what it's like to accompany a person with Parkinson's. It is a sore trial—for Jeannene, for obvious reasons, but also for Jim. And yet, there was light in his eyes. "This is what I signed up for," he said to me over coffee. "It's hard. But I'm happy to do it."

Tranquility and wisdom and high holiness radiated from Jim, resolved as he is not to deny the reality of encroaching death but to stare it in the eye and even extend to it the hospitality made possible by the Passion of Christ—a hospitality enabling Jim and Jeannene to gather themselves and decide carefully how to live the life they would love—a life full of gentleness and grace and confident hope. And though they would surely welcome divine healing, they know that nothing—not even death itself—can separate them from the love of God that is in Christ Jesus our Lord (Romans 8:39).

They have come to rest in this. They have hung all their hopes on it.

I believe now, by theological conviction and by long experience, that because of what Jesus has done, Christians have literally nothing to fear in the heavens or on the earth. In descending from the heights to our depths, he's filled it all. The unthinkable privilege—indeed, all the joy—of our work as the people of God is to declare it to whomever we can, as often as we can. "We glory in your cross, O Lord," says the Good Friday acclamation in *The Book of Common Prayer*, "for by virtue of your cross, joy has come to the whole world."[18]

I clung to those words the day I got a call from a man in my congregation named Roy. He and his wife Betty are in their late seventies. Their adult daughter Julie had spent several years struggling with cancer and was in her final hours. They asked if I'd come pray.

When I arrived, the family was gathered around Julie's bed. Though she was unconscious and struggling for breath, several members were at pains to insist that Julie could still hear, and that if I had something to say directly to her, I should say it.

With that, I sat by Julie on the bed, anointed her with oil, and began to pray—loud enough for her to hear. "Jesus," I began, "you lived and died as one of us. You made our death yours. You are here. I pray that you would minister to Julie's spirit even as we speak. Help her know that you are with her, and that it's safe to let go—that you'll carry her in death just as surely as you've carried her in life. And help her know that you'll carry her family in her absence as well. Please help everyone here—Julie included—to trust you in life and death."

After the prayer and a few more minutes of visiting, I said goodbye and left to help lead an evening worship service.

Later that night I got a text from Roy: "Pastor Andrew, what you prayed over Julie she must have heard—she passed away twenty minutes after you left. Thank you for coming."

"Thank you for having me," I said. It was my privilege. It always is.

SAFE WITH JESUS

I'd like to believe that Roy was right—that Julie heard me saying that she was safe with Jesus, and that her family was safe with Jesus, and that therefore it was okay to go. I suppose at the Great Renewal, if I get a free minute, I'll ask her and find out.

Either way, after nearly twenty years of pastoring, I'm more convinced than ever that this is central not only to my calling as a pastor but to *our* calling as God's people—announcing God to the depths. As Betsie Ten Boom, sister of the Holocaust survivor Corrie Ten Boom, said from her deathbed, "There is no pit so deep that He is not deeper still."[19] Because of Jesus' descent into the shadow of death, we know that there is a deep beyond the deep—and that the Deep is safe, because the Deep is Jesus, and Jesus is good.

In his commentary on the book of Jonah, scholar Phillip Cary writes of the reluctant prophet's descent into the belly of the fish. There, Jonah discovers "a deep beyond the deep, beyond the furthest limits of the world." This lesson is for us, too. For "what is deeper than the depths and before the beginning of the world and beyond its end is the word of the LORD who created them and you, who keeps faith with the people of his covenant."[20]

Gustavo Gutiérrez agrees, writing that after Job discovers God at the very bottom of his suffering, he learns that "the unknown is no longer a monster that threatens to devour everything." Gutiérrez then quotes a prayer of Luís Espinal, a murdered Bolivian priest: "Train us, Lord, to fling ourselves upon the impossible, for behind the impossible is your grace and your presence; we cannot fall into emptiness."[21]

Fall as far as you may, the prayer tells us—you will fall, safe and secure, right into the hands of our good God.

Today's neuroscientists are teaching us that a sense of safety is no small thing; indeed, it is the most fundamental human need. The things that make us human—our ability to laugh and play, to connect and relate, to sing and dance and create—will remain "offline" or severely underdeveloped until we know in our bones that we are safe with one another. Fear diminishes us.

The gospel tells us that in Christ Jesus, "safe" is precisely what we are. That he, the human God, made us and loves us and is our companion in life and in death. That he means us no harm. And that he will never do us harm. And that he will hold us in every wonderful and horrible thing life will throw at us until he leads us finally—*safely*—into the kingdom of his Father, who is also our Father, where sin and death and fear will be no more.

The psalmist said, "He who dwells in the secret place of the Most High shall abide under the shadow of the Almighty" (Psalm 91:1 NKJV).

Jesus is the secret place.

And his shadow is the shadow cast by his cross.

Chapter 5

QUESTIONS FOR DISCUSSION

1. Where have you experienced the destructive effects of death-denial?

2. If those affected by that experience were to embrace the notion that because of what Jesus did, death is not to be feared, how might things change?

3. Where do you need to know a sense of safety with Jesus?

6

EASTER

The Future Does Not Depend on Us

Son of man, can these bones live?
—EZEKIEL 37:3

I am neither an optimist nor a pessimist; Jesus Christ is risen from the dead.
—LESSLIE NEWBIGIN

Spring 1965. A group of protestors begins a march from Selma to Montgomery to draw national attention to the state of Alabama's resistance to the Civil Rights Act of 1964. The protestors had been warned by Alabama's governor that the march would not be tolerated. Government threats notwithstanding, nearly six hundred folks show up to march in peaceful protest.

When they reach the edge of Selma at the Edmund Pettus Bridge, they meet state resistance head-on. The commanding officer orders the protestors to disband, and before long troopers are shoving the demonstrators, firing tear gas into the crowd, beating them with clubs, even trampling them on mounted horseback.

The march achieved its goal, eliciting a swift denunciation from the White House, which led to the subsequent passage of the Voting Rights Act, a landmark piece of legislation. What came to be known as Bloody Sunday was a watershed moment in our nation's history.

A man by the name of John Lewis was among the protestors that day. He was twenty-five. Born and raised in Troy, Alabama, Lewis—who later became an ordained minister—had been drawn into the civil rights movement after hearing the testimony of Rosa Parks and the preaching of Dr. King. He was instrumental in the leadership of the events of Bloody Sunday and was among the first to be brutalized by state troopers. He suffered a skull fracture and was fortunate to survive.

Over the next decades, Lewis's leadership would continue to rise, with dozens of imprisonments for civil disobedience interspersed amongst his tireless efforts as a Georgia state representative to help King's vision of "the beloved community" come into being. At a 2000 dinner honoring Congressman Lewis, President Bill Clinton remarked that Lewis's courage in the face of adversity on Bloody Sunday "freed me too."[1]

Righteous action is like that. Makes chains fall off.

John Lewis passed away in 2020. Several years before he died, in an interview with radio journalist Krista Tippet, he was asked about the source of his remarkable endurance in the face of opposition. In the recording, Lewis replies, "You had to have a sense of faith *that what you were moving towards was already done . . . that it had already happened.*"

The moment catches Tippet off guard. She asks him to say more. Replies Lewis:

"You live as though you're already there."[2]

As though you're already there . . .

I can hardly think of a better segue into the meaning of Easter.

CAN THESE BONES LIVE?

Where do Christians find the strength to endure amid suffocating hopelessness?

The prophet Ezekiel knew the threat of hopelessness. When the Babylonians sacked Jerusalem around the turn of the sixth-century BCE, he found himself among the deportees. The psalmist captured the grim mood of those exiles: "By the rivers of Babylon we sat and wept when we remembered Zion" (Psalm 137:1).

Lamenting what had been, anxious about what will be, and wondering how to carry on—what do you do when life falls to pieces and your agency seems to have run its course?

You could let mourning give way to feelings of vengeance, as the psalmist did, as many do:

> Daughter Babylon, doomed to destruction,
>   happy is the one who repays you
>   according to what you have done to us.
> Happy is the one who seizes your infants
>   and dashes them against the rocks. (Psalm 137:8–9)

Or . . . you could be like Ezekiel: "While I was among the exiles by the Kebar River," the prophet writes, "the heavens were opened and I saw visions of God" (Ezekiel 1:1).

Sometimes, you just have to see God. Nothing else will do.

The visions unfold in wild detail for the prophet until the pivotal moment. Staring out at a valley of dry bones, the Lord asks: "Son of man, can these bones live?" (Ezekiel 37:3).

It is the Lord who asks, but God is really echoing the question that burned at the center of every living Israelite's soul. Ezekiel is brutally honest: "Sovereign LORD, you alone know," he says.

Only God really knows if we have a future.

And so God begins to speak to Ezekiel. "Talk to the bones," he says. Ezekiel does, and the very dry bones are joined together, clothed in flesh, and re-spirited, becoming a vast multitude.

The people will live because God wills that they live. They will have a future because God wills that they have a future, for theirs is the Lord of Life.

Can these bones live? is not only Israel's question but ours. Robert Jenson writes that for Ezekiel and the other deportees, the exile "seems to have brought Israel to its end. Thus the Lord's question to Ezekiel, 'Has death won?' . . . Israel's question is really the question that every people eventually asks: 'Does death win? Does life have any other point other than its own refutation?'"

Sometimes, when surveying the wreckage of our world, our lives, it seems like the answer must surely be, "No, it does not. Death has the final say."

And then the strange and gracious light of the gospel comes along, illuminating the good will of God behind the wreckage. "The Christian church claims that Jesus' resurrection is the Lord's answer to this question."[3]

God asks, "Can the bones live?"

We respond, "Only you know."

And Jesus walks out of the grave.

RUBBLE AND PROMISES

When the Son took up residence in the womb of Mary, the destiny of humanity and the destiny of Jesus became inextricably intertwined. Just as his life simply *is* our life and his death *is* our death, so also his resurrection simply *is* our own (1 Corinthians 15:20–22). I find that an unspeakable source of comfort: that God promises a future to us, and indeed that promise is sure, because Christ is raised.

Of course, that has taken me a long time to learn.

About a decade ago, a church I was pastoring went through a season of leadership turmoil that left it, and us, eviscerated. My wife and I had been in the saddle for five years, had worked hard, and had seen the Spirit work wonders, building up a vibrant community in a difficult environment. Every inch gained we cherished as a precious gift.

And then the turmoil. When the dust settled, half of our staff and leadership were gone. Rumors swirled. Many congregants left, while those who remained were deeply shaken by what had happened. The atmosphere of optimism that had once been ours suddenly became a nearly smothering cloud of uncertainty. I wasn't sure how or if we would survive, and I was severely depleted by the conflict.

It was my family's habit to head up to central Wisconsin after Christmas to be with our extended families and take some time to recuperate and reset for the coming year. I had always approached those trips with expectation—a chance to get away, get some perspective, listen to the voice of God, and prepare to reengage my work. Part of my process was to sneak off to a coffee shop for several hours on New Year's Eve to journal my reflections on the past year and to outline how I sensed the Lord leading us into the future.

We did the same this year—except that this time, I approached my reflective time with dread. Sitting at a table in the back of the coffee shop, I wrote: "The end of the year . . . I hurt so badly . . . I did my best to make decisions that I thought were honoring to everyone . . . but no matter how hard I tried to do it right, it got more and more complicated until eventually it became a cancerous growth that metastasized and nearly killed us all. I want to be 'over it,' but I'm not. It still hurts so badly . . . and I wonder if our church is doomed to die a meaningless and futile death."

That was about the most I could muster. I sighed heavily as I wrote. Tears fell. Some, anyway. But even that was a weight—the weight of knowing the grief was more profound than the moment could create space for, but that I *needed* to grieve, desperately. There would be more tears to come.

Or would there? Are there some sadnesses that are simply unreachable? That too was a weight. I didn't know.

Amid all that, a horrifying thought dawned: *I have to preach next weekend*—the first weekend of the new year. What on earth was I supposed to say after all we had gone through?

"For we do not preach ourselves, but Christ Jesus the Lord, and ourselves your bondservants for Jesus' sake," writes Paul (2 Corinthians 4:5 NKJV). As a pastor, I remind myself often that my first task is not to offer an exposition of my inner life; nor is it to wax eloquent on the level of my personal optimism about the future—it's to read the Bible and serve up a hearty helping of the promises to people starved to know that God is for them.

On a hunch, I decided to turn to the Revised Common Lectionary—a table of scripture readings for the church year used by Christians around the world. I'd done that here and there over the years and was always astonished at how fitting the readings tended to be. This time proved no exception.

Among the readings for the first Sunday of the new year was this doozy from Jeremiah. To a group of people whose lives had been reduced to ash by the exile, the Lord said, "I have loved you with an everlasting love; I have drawn you with unfailing kindness. I will build you up again, and you, Virgin Israel, will be rebuilt" (Jeremiah 31:3–4). Given my church's situation, the audacity of the prophet's words struck me with peculiar force. How does Jeremiah have the chutzpah to say something like this? Nothing in Israel's experience at that moment would have indicated anything like a great rebuilding to come.

But of course, I knew the answer right away—as you probably do as well: *Jeremiah can say this because he knows God—the God who makes promises and keeps them.* Covenant is the alpha and omega of Israel's life. And ours.

Jeremiah is not calculating the future of Israel based upon observable facts. He is wagering in the confidence born of faith. The "weeping prophet" pushes all his chips to the middle of the table, betting on God.

And that was just the word I needed—a promise over the rubble of the life of our church.

I preached on that very text the following Sunday and was astonished by the permission it granted me. It allowed me to tell all the truth I could about our situation and still speak a word of hope. I could—and did—say, "On the human level, I am bruised and battered right along with you, and I have very little hope"—and then, in the same breath—"but our future together does not depend on us. It depends on God. And God is faithful. Let's keep going."

A REBUKE TO DESPAIR

"I am neither an optimist nor a pessimist; Jesus Christ is risen from the dead," the great missiologist Lesslie Newbigin famously said near the end of his life.[4] Faith, as I have often told congregations I have pastored, is not a rational calculation based on present circumstance. It's not *optimism*—looking at the facts and saying, "I think we've got a pretty good shot here."

No, it's none of that. Faith is what the writer of Hebrews described as "the substance of things hoped for, the evidence of things not seen" (Hebrews 11:1 NKJV). Faith is a concrete manifestation of the very future that God has promised us, and it is so precisely, according to the writer of Hebrews, because the Crucified One is raised (Hebrews 2:8–9).

Another way of saying this is that the future is actual, is *real*, because Jesus lives. Remember John Lewis: "You had to have a sense of faith that what you were moving towards *was already done . . . that it had already happened.*" In Jesus, *the future has happened*, it is here and now, and we have access to it as we have access to him (2 Corinthians 5:17).

The message of Easter is therefore a rebuke to every form of despair. And despair *is* deadly. The late medieval poet Dante understood this, which is why the superscription over the gates of his imagined hell read, "Abandon hope, all ye who enter here." The loss of hope is quite literally hell. We cannot live without it.

The Holocaust survivor Viktor Frankl saw the deadliness of despair firsthand in the Nazi death camps. A highly regarded Austrian psychiatrist, Frankl came to see that hope was crucial for a person's entire well-being; that without something to live for, people literally fall apart. "The prisoner who had lost faith in the future—his future—was doomed. With his loss of belief in the future, he also lost his spiritual hold; he let himself decline and become subject to mental and physical decay."[5]

Hope, for Frankl, was decidedly *not* optimism. He tells the story of a man whose hope was buoyed by a dream in which the longed-for liberation would come on a specific day in March. The day came, without liberation. The very next day, the man was dead. "To all outward appearances, he had died of typhus," writes Frankl. "[But] the ultimate cause of my friend's death was that the expected liberation did not come and he was severely disappointed. This suddenly lowered his body's resistance against the latent typhus infection. His faith in the future and his will to live had become paralyzed and his body fell victim to illness."[6]

Cause of death: despair. Imagine that. Frankl's testimony demonstrates with peculiar force why we can't place our hope in this or that outcome, delivered on this or that day. It needs to be in something firmer, more solid. It needs to be in Christ. As the old hymn goes, because Christ lives, "all fear is gone."[7]

To speak the gospel is to keep telling people this—against all the brutal facticity of their moment. Such telling does not imply a *denial* of the facts. Jürgen Moltmann says that Christian faith "sees in the resurrection of Christ not the eternity of heaven"—that is, a promise of escape, which is a form of despair—"*but the future of the very earth on which his cross stands.*"[8]

We can tell (and help others tell) the God's-honest truth about this broken earth without succumbing to despair because in Christ we have seen the Murdered One taken up into life. The Second Person forever bears the scars of our history in his body, and we are made wise when with Thomas we respond to the Risen One's invitation to "put your finger here; see my hands. Reach out your hand and put it into my side" (John 20:27).

Faith in Jesus Christ allows us to look our situations in the eye without flinching. We have to be honest about the brutal facts—about the many places where sin has damaged and distorted our world. "Unless we understand the very depths of our corruption [and] misery," writes scholar Susannah

Heschel, "the hope we offer is superficial." And yet, she cautions, we must not despair, for "to despair is to deny that God is present."[9] To "be honest" without considering the great fact of the resurrection is not to tell all the truth; in fact, it is to lay the groundwork for cynicism and despair. "Be joyful // though you have considered all the facts," counsels Wendell Berry.[10]

What Easter finally teaches is that as the risen Jesus is God's yes over the life of the cosmos, so also is he God's yes over each of our lives. The Resurrected One bears scars, yes—but the Crucified One is now raised. Death does not have the final say. "Pastoral work," Eugene Peterson reminds us—and I think that this is true for *all believers at all times*—"consists in repeating the gospel yes in every conceivable life situation and encouraging the yes answer of faith."[11]

In Christ, the yes of the Father prevails. Forever. And that yes gives us courage to act boldly even in the face of despair. "Hope of the resurrection is in no sense an evasion of concrete history," writes Gustavo Gutiérrez. "On the contrary, it leads to a redoubling of effort in the struggle against what brings unjust death."[12]

ANSWERING FAITH

On Easter Sunday, I told my congregation that Christ was raised, and they sang their amens like R. S. Thomas said they would, fiercely and with faith. The next Sunday at our church was Baptism Sunday, and we baptized a whole mess of folk.

I cried and I cried as I watched them line up at the front of the auditorium to declare their faith, for many of them had very good reasons not to be there. A young man who just passed through the fires of a painful faith deconstruction. A young woman who has spent years wrestling with suicidal ideation and self-harm. An older man whose life nearly bottomed out completely from substance abuse and addiction.

I looked each one in the eye and told them that God in Christ was for them and not against them, that the one whom Jesus called Father was now also their Father and was raising them to new life, and that because nothing the Father intends will finally fail, what was happening in those waters was a miracle that could never be undone.

Each came up dripping wet as tears rolled down my cheeks. The words of the psalmist rang in my ears: "The LORD has done this, and it is marvelous in our eyes" (Psalm 118:23). I'll never get over it. The yes of the Father prevails.

Among the worshipers in the baptismal service was the woman married to the man with the pornography addiction whom I'd met with several months earlier. For many months now she'd been coming. I had watched her strength increase as she heard, week after week, the good news about Jesus who died and rose to life again and is not only the future of the world but her future, too. It was inspiring.

Not long ago she laid an ultimatum down for her husband. When he did not rise to the occasion, she made good her word and kicked him out. She told me it was the hardest thing she'd ever done, and I didn't doubt it. She second-guessed herself sometimes, as we all do when we have to make hard choices. *Was it the right thing? Wouldn't it be easier if I let him come home? How will I provide for myself and my child if the marriage ends?* Anxious, trembling questions—not unlike the first witnesses in Mark's resurrection account: "Trembling and bewildered, the women went out and fled from the tomb. They said nothing to anyone, because they were afraid" (Mark 16:8).

Sometimes, "trembling and bewildered" is about the best we can muster in the face of the promise.

Even still, all the questions notwithstanding, I could see how faith in the One who lives beyond death is making her alive. Her countenance and demeanor were different. She walked straighter. Spoke with more confidence. Held her head higher. There was light in her eyes and growing joy in her heart.

Because he lives.

PROPHETS OF A FUTURE NOT OUR OWN

Easter helps us make sense of the place that our efforts occupy in the grand scheme of God, teaching us to understand the relationship between our work and God's.

I preached the book of Revelation a couple of years ago. What struck me most forcibly was that in John's vision of the End, the future that God has promised descends out of heaven to earth as a pure, unearned, utterly unmerited gift of grace. After all the tumult of our age, God makes good his word. The kingdom comes.

The future, John is saying, is God's doing, not ours.

I find that a nearly unspeakable source of comfort. When I first started out in ministry, I remember hearing a lot of talk among church leaders about our obligation to "build the kingdom" and "establish the kingdom" and "grow the kingdom." As a young pastor, I found talk like that energizing, so I set to work trying to "build the kingdom" and such.

The thing was, I couldn't ever tell if I was doing it. My efforts seemed so small, so paltry, so prone to wash away in the waters of circumstance. Did that mean that the kingdom was therefore small and paltry and washaway-able? Or maybe I wasn't doing it right, wasn't working hard enough. I didn't know.

The anxiety that notion created was quite nearly crushing. Then one day I ran into a poem written in tribute to the late archbishop of El Salvador, Oscar Romero. Romero, a champion for the poor and oppressed in Latin America, was shot to death in church in the early 1980s while presiding over the eucharist. Almost immediately, he became something of an icon—a symbol of what Dietrich Bonhoeffer had called "costly discipleship." The poem written in his honor situates the relationship between our efforts and God's exactly the way I think it ought to be situated:

> We plant the seeds that one day will grow.
> We water seeds already planted, knowing that they hold future promise.
> We lay foundations that will need further development.
> We provide yeast that produces far beyond our capabilities.
> We cannot do everything, and there is a sense of liberation in realizing that.
> This enables us to do something, and to do it very well.
> It may be incomplete, but it is a beginning, a step along the way, an opportunity for the Lord's grace to enter and do the rest.
> We may never see the end results, but that is the difference between the master builder and the worker.
> We are workers, not master builders; ministers, not messiahs.
> We are prophets of a future not our own.[13]

So: Where do Christians find the strength to endure amid suffocating hopelessness? Where do we find the resolve to act in the face of encroaching despair?

The answer is quite simply *God*—the God who raised Jesus from the dead. Easter is God's self-identification, God's calling card. It's what God does, who God *is*. As Jenson says, in one of his more memorable lines: God is "whoever raised Jesus from the dead."[14]

And so we cry out—*with* Jesus who was raised, *to* the Father who raised him—"Thy kingdom come, thy will be done, on earth as it is in heaven," trusting God, and not ourselves, to make all things new.

Chapter 6

QUESTIONS FOR DISCUSSION

1. How have you typically thought about Easter, whether from lessons learned in childhood or more recently? How has this chapter shifted or filled out your understanding of Easter?

2. Describe a time in your life when you've found hope and courage in the resurrection. Is there a place in your life now where you need to experience hope?

ASCENSION

To the Heart of Things

And God raised us up with Christ and seated us with him
in the heavenly realms in Christ Jesus.
—EPHESIANS 2:6

We saw him go and yet we were not parted,
He took us with him to the heart of things.
—MALCOM GUITE, "Ascension Day"

The average churchgoer may go their entire lives without
hearing a message on the ascension of Jesus Christ. But
there it is in the Nicene Creed, driven like a nail into the
household of our salvation: "He ascended into heaven . . . ."

The ascension is part and parcel of the strange light of the
story of Jesus and is present, explicitly or implicitly, whenever
that story is told.

Nor is it simply *a* part of the story—a take-it-or-leave-it
add-on—but rather an *inextricable* part, as Calvin points out:
"For although Christ, by rising again, began fully to display
his glory and virtue, having laid aside the abject and ignoble
condition of a mortal life, and the ignominy of the cross, *yet*

it was only by his ascension to heaven that his reign is truly commenced."[1]

If Calvin is correct, then even with the resurrection, we still do not have a completed work of salvation. You can't say "good news" without saying "he ascended." The Son Crucified and Raised must also be the Son Ascended, or we are still lost.

On the face of it, the ascension does not seem like very good news. Luke tells us that after his resurrection, Jesus spent forty days with his disciples, eating and drinking and teaching, rather like he did in the years prior to his crucifixion. And the natural question followed: "Lord, are you at this time going to restore the kingdom to Israel?" (Acts 1:6). As usual, Jesus demurred, and then "was taken up before their very eyes, and a cloud hid him from their sight" (Acts 1:9).

And this is supposed to be good news? Robert Farrar Capon notices the oddity of the ascension and considers it of one piece with the overall tenor of the gospel: After all his work, Jesus "simply disappeared" writes Capon, "leaving—as far as anybody has been able to see in the two thousand or so years since—no apparent city, no effective kingdom able to make the world straighten up and fly right." It's all mystery, he says. "The whole operation began as a mystery, continued as a mystery, came to fruition as a mystery, and to this day continues to function as a mystery."[2]

The story of God-with-us never ceases to be strange.

The ascension has often been the subject of Christian art, much of it, quite frankly, hilarious and itself a bit strange— Jesus flying up into the heavens with little more than a loincloth draped precariously across his midsection, surrounded by the cherubim (who are, naturally, usually depicted as naked flying babies), his mother and disciples looking on below in bewilderment.

The trope repeats itself across the ages in various forms. My favorite depictions of the ascension, and I think the funniest, are those where the only part of Jesus that is in view is his *feet*—the caboose of a body that has, so it seems, not yet pulled all the way into its heavenly station.

But the art, whether ridiculous or sublime, is telling us some things we need to know about what God has done for us in Christ, how the world is new now that the man Jesus who is God is raised from the dead and seated at the right hand of the Father.

GOD ENTHRONED

The words of the psalmist set the theological agenda of the ascension for us:

> Clap your hands, all you nations;
> > shout to God with cries of joy.
> For the LORD Most High is awesome,
> > the great King over all the earth.
> He subdued nations under us,
> > peoples under our feet.
> He chose our inheritance for us,
> > the pride of Jacob, whom he loved.
>
> God has ascended amid shouts of joy,
> > the LORD amid the sounding of trumpets.
> Sing praises to God, sing praises;
> > sing praises to our King, sing praises.
> For God is the King of all the earth;
> > sing to him a psalm of praise. (Psalm 47:1–7)

The psalm pictures Israel's God as a warrior-king, descending into the morass of human chaos, subduing it, and re-ascending from there to his throne amid shouts of joy. Israel and the nations worship together as the covenant people:

God reigns over the nations;
    God is seated on his holy throne.
The nobles of the nations assemble
    as the people of the God of Abraham,
for the kings of the earth belong to God;
    he is greatly exalted. (Psalm 47:8–9)

It took no great stretch of the imagination for the early church to see in texts like this the career of the Christ, the Second Person who likewise descended into the chaos of our age, subdued the powers by his death and resurrection, and commenced his reign at the Father's right hand by his ascension into heaven, Jew and Gentile made one united, worshiping people by the power of the Holy Spirit. This was precisely Peter's message to the astonished onlookers at Pentecost:

Exalted to the right hand of God, [Jesus] has received from the Father the promised Holy Spirit and has poured out what you now see and hear. For David did not ascend to heaven, and yet he said,

"The Lord said to my Lord:
    'Sit at my right hand
until I make your enemies
    a footstool for your feet.'"

Therefore let all Israel be assured of this: God has made this Jesus, whom you crucified, both Lord and Messiah. (Acts 2:33–36)

The ascension, therefore, is about *that*—the exaltation of this man, Jesus Christ, as the Messiah of Israel and Lord of the world. He is God-in-flesh who has ascended to universal rule amid shouts of joy, settling the question once and for all, "Who's in charge?"

WHAT GOD IS UP TO

"Who's in charge?" is a crucial question, both existentially and practically, for it is an inescapable fact that the world operates by authority structures; so close are they to our lived existence that for the most part we hardly notice them, like fish in water or birds in the sky—that is, until something goes awry. Recall the last time you had a dispute with an insurance agent about what your policy does and does not cover, or the last time your meal at a favorite restaurant got botched and the words "Can I talk to whoever is in charge here?" cascaded effortlessly from your lips.

The world runs on authority—though we are often at pains to deny it. I sat with a congregant who came of age during the great cultural revolution of the 1960s and '70s. He described how the allergy to authority in those post-WWII days was so great that in many circles, the absolute freedom promised by anarchy seemed like the only real possibility for human flourishing. But of course, the anarchic impulse, however much it may promise freedom from "the man," only substitutes one form of authority (mob rule) for another (the runaway state).

Someone is in charge, and something in our bones tells us that it is critical we know who that is, what they are like, and whether their authority is valid.

The anxiety recurs in every age and cuts across ideological and political lines. I was a boy growing up in a religiously and politically conservative congregation when President Clinton was elected to his first term. I can vividly remember how "the sky is falling" rhetoric surged through our community. Years later, I was pastoring a rather more "blue" church when President Trump was elected, and I can vividly recall how fear for the future constricted the hearts of so many of my congregants.

I remember taking note of this, and marveling at it—that however different the social location, the anxieties were strikingly similar. I say this not to minimize anyone's concerns but to note how kindred and recurrent those concerns are. Across my years of ministry, I've tried hard to reassure my congregations that the words of Lady Julian of Norwich are true for all time: "All shall be well, and all shall be well, and all manner of thing shall be well"[3]—no matter whom the American president happens to be.

Christians, of course, can say *all shall be well, and all shall be well, and all manner of thing shall be well* precisely because we believe that Jesus Christ is raised from death and exalted to the right hand of the Father, clothed in omnipotence, subduing the powers—as Paul writes in 1 Corinthians 15: "For he must reign until he has put all enemies under his feet" (verse 25).

So if you ask the question "What is God up to?" *that* is your answer, *that* is what is happening in the universe. Jesus is reigning. God is in charge. The world is being guided to a good end.

JESUS REIGNS

November 2015 was a tumultuous month. Unrest in Romania, an Islamic State terrorist attack in Paris, retaliatory strikes in Raqqa, Syria (then a key headquartering location for the Islamic State), and the siege of a hotel in Mali by Islamic extremists.

The church I pastored was shaken. As ever, I wondered what to do. And the lectionary scripture readings came to the rescue. Yet again.

I'd been wondering what to say about all these troubling things and how to say it. And then the last Sunday after Pentecost, Christ the King Sunday, rolled up and said, "Here you go, preacher. Preach this."

The texts couldn't possibly have been more apropos to the moment: Daniel's vision of the wild beasts whose flesh-devouring reign is terminated by the Ancient of Days (Daniel 7:14). The psalmist's conviction that the Lord who reigns is mightier than the thundering of the waters (Psalm 93). The Apocalypse in which the risen Jesus is declared to be "the ruler of the kings of the earth" (Revelation 1:4–5). And straight through to the gospel of John where Pilate stammers and quails before the man from Nazareth of Galilee who says to him, "My kingdom is not of this world" (John 18:36).

That'll do, I thought. *Those texts will be just fine, thanks*. I spent the week meditating on them. And wove them together with some remarks on the uncertainty and even terror we all had been experiencing. And then said to that little flock what I knew Jesus would want me to say to them, what I think the risen Jesus is *always* saying to all of us: "Do not be afraid"— which is, after all, the most frequently repeated command in Scripture.

What I remember most about that Sunday was a sense of well-being wrapping us up like a warm blanket. "Jesus reigns," I told them. "Our world is held by strong hands. We can trust this." I could see faith rising in their eyes, comfort surrounding their hearts.

That day, the Ascended Jesus walked the room.

WE GO WITH HIM

The ascension is good news because it teaches us that God reigns by his Christ.

If that were all it said, surely it would be enough. But it says more, for as often as the writers of the Epistles speak of the ascension in terms of the reign of God, they also make curious comments like this one from Paul to the Ephesians: "And God raised us up with Christ and seated us with him in the heavenly realms in Christ Jesus" (Ephesians 2:6).

It is not just *Jesus* who ascends to the heavens—*we also ascend with him.* Somehow, the Scriptures tell us, our flesh is so united to him that *whatever happens to him happens to us.* When Jesus goes to heaven, ascending forever into the direct presence of God, he does not leave us behind. We go with him.

But whatever can this mean?

In the evangelicalism of my upbringing (and still to this day), salvation was often positioned as the offer to "go to heaven to be with Jesus when you die." Services often ended with the question, "If you died tonight, do you know where you'd spend eternity?"

The theology of that way of talking has been rightly critiqued in recent years, with theologians and scholars noting that the New Testament nowhere positions salvation as the offer to go to heaven and be with Jesus when you die. Rather, the offer is "repent and be baptized . . . in the name of Jesus Christ for the forgiveness of your sins" (Acts 2:38), whereupon the baptized join the church in the life of salvation.

Please, then, no more talk of "going to heaven to be with Jesus when you die," right?

Well, I say not so fast. If we're following the New Testament, I think we have to say that the problem with "going to heaven to be with Jesus when you die" theology isn't so much the notion itself but what we mean by the notion and where we put it in the story of salvation—an offer for the very *end* of our lives, and that to some disembodied, disincarnate realm, rather than an invitation *for the very beginning of new life within the confines of this very life.* Listen to Paul elsewhere, in a passage that dovetails nicely with Ephesians 2:6:

> Don't you know that all of us who were baptized into Christ Jesus were baptized into his death? We were there-fore buried with him through baptism into death in order that, just as Christ was raised from the dead through the glory of the Father, we too may live a new life. (Romans 6:3–4)

For Paul, to be baptized is not to accept the offer to go to heaven to be with Jesus when we die *one day*; rather, to be baptized is to *accept the offer to die and go to heaven to be with Jesus right now,* inside the very conditions of our lives. Paul's remarks to the Colossian believers tell the tale:

> Since, then, you have been raised with Christ, set your hearts on things above, where Christ is, seated at the right hand of God. Set your minds on things above, not on earthly things. For you died, and your life is now hidden with Christ in God. When Christ, who is your life, appears, then you also will appear with him in glory. (Colossians 3:1–4)

Our life and his—bound together, never to be separated. When he goes to heaven, ascending to the right hand of his Father, we go with him—to be where he is, *even as we remain in this world.* The English poet Malcom Guite gets it exactly right in his "Ascension Day" sonnet when he writes:

We saw him go and yet we were not parted,
He took us with him to the heart of things.[4]

Karl Barth and John Calvin made this New Testament pattern a centerpiece of their respective theologies. For Barth, the counterpart to the humiliation of the Son of God was none other than the exaltation of the Son of Man. Note the accent marks of his theology: "It is God who went into the far country" to seek and save the lost, he writes, "and it is man who returns home. *Both took place in Jesus Christ.*"[5] Likewise, Calvin (whom Barth learned a great deal from): "The Lord, by his ascension to heaven, has opened up the access to the heavenly kingdom, which Adam had shut. For having entered it in our flesh, as it were in our name, it follows, as the apostle says, that we are in a manner now seated in heavenly places, *not entertaining a mere hope of heaven, but possessing it in our head*"[6]—that is, in Christ.

For Calvin, the ascension teaches us that heaven is not out there somewhere but is right here and right now and that we are in it with Jesus in the midst of this world because of what he has done for us.

Theologian Julie Canlis notes that for Calvin, the ascension was "the foundation of his doctrine of *participation*"— that is, *communion*, or the way in which the human Jesus incorporates us into his life as a member of the Trinity, thereby deepening our connection not only to God but to one another.[7] The ascension of Jesus, in other words, doesn't take us *out* of this world, but takes us *further into* God and *further into* the heart of the world. It drives us into participation, into koinonia, into deeper mutuality and life-giving fellowship. And that is because the ascension of Jesus didn't take him out of this world but instead deepened his fellowship with it. "He who descended is the very one who ascended higher than all the heavens, in order to fill the whole universe" (Ephesians 4:10).

To live in the power of the ascension is to live in ever-intensifying relationship—with God, with the created order, with those around us. As Guite says, "*He took us with him to the heart of things.*"

Ascension, therefore, is not about Jesus going *away* from us, exacerbating the separations created by sin; rather, ascension is about *Christ drawing ever-nearer to us, and us ever-nearer to Christ*—it is about the transfiguration of our humanity by way of participation in God, a transfiguration that influences every area of our lives, most especially our relationships with others. "The new being produced by baptism is a new *person*, a new being-in-relation," writes Catherine LaCugna. "Those who identify with Jesus in baptism are given a new way of being in the world, now as fully personal. Putting on Christ . . . becomes the authentic basis for a true communion among persons."

As we trust that this is so, so also does it become visible. We become a "sign in the world of this new existence."[8]

ICON OF CHRIST

I stood gaping at the image at the National Gallery in London: the seventeenth-century Spanish painter Bartolomé Esteban Murillo's depiction of the crucified Christ reaching down from his cross to embrace a young man who looks up to him in adoration and devotion. The painting is a representation of the calling of one of my favorite figures from church history—Saint Francis of Assisi.

Francis has always moved me. His joy, his simplicity, his love for the poor and for the created order, his dedication to the cause of Jesus which is the cause of peace. Francis burned with holiness. A man on fire.

Many in our day find Francis moving and inspiring. In an era where the gap between rich and poor continues to widen, where environmental catastrophe threatens to engulf us, and where our love of power and dread of "the other" manifests in constant social strife, Francis and his legacy offer a way forward.

Yet it is my impression that what is too often lost in the veneration of Francis is *where* his peculiar goodness came from—and Murillo's piece leaves us with no doubt: it is *from Christ* that Francis's saintliness derives.

For Murillo, Francis was not an icon of simplicity or humility or love for nature or humanity per se—he was, in the most technical and literal sense, *an icon of Christ*, a fact borne witness to by the many pieces at the National Gallery exhibit. In depictions of Francis from medieval times to today, the man of Assisi begins to look more and more like Christ himself as Francis grows in grace, the two personalities merging into one.

You can't, in other words, make sense of Francis without invoking the name of the Christ, who in every way precedes and surpasses him.

For it is Christ who made Francis and Christ who elevated Francis and Christ who drove Francis to his wild acts of generosity and humility and self-sacrifice, and it is Christ we see in Francis who in a euphoric ecstasy flung himself into Christ and submerged himself into Christ and lost himself in Christ and just thereby lit up the world with the radiant love and light of the God we see first and always in Christ.

Francis, that beautiful beggar, sat on the throne with Christ as a king in the midst of this world, showing us what it means to be human like Jesus is human.

And that is why we love and remember Saint Francis—not for his sake, because we met and still meet *Christ* in him.

THE FULLNESS OF HIM WHO FILLS

That is quite simply what the story of Jesus is all about—the way in which God by his Christ gathers us up to himself and glorifies us with him in the midst of this world. Theologian Khaled Anatolios explains that "the full manifestation of Jesus' retrieval of the divine glory comes about in the ascension, when his humanity is fully integrated into the divine glory." But remember—Jesus' humanity is *ours*, and ours is *his*. Which means that when Christ ascends, our humanity becomes "a full participant in the divine glory and is fully reintegrated into the intra-trinitarian glorification."[9]

We become, in other words, through Christ's ascension, *all we were ever meant to be*.

But what does that mean, practically speaking? Anatolios draws attention to the transforming effect of discovering our lives hidden with Christ in God by quoting this bit of liturgy from the Eastern Orthodox tradition:

> Knowing the commandments of the Lord, let this be our way of life: let us feed the hungry, let us give the thirsty drink, let us clothe the naked, let us welcome strangers, let us visit those in prison and the sick. Then the Judge of all the earth will say even to us: "Come, you blessed of my Father, inherit the Kingdom prepared for you."
>
> While fasting with the body, brothers, and sisters, let us also fast in spirit. Let us loose every bond of iniquity; let us undo the knots of every contract made by violence; let us tear up all unjust agreements; let us give bread to the hungry and welcome to our house the poor who have no

roof to cover them, that we may receive great mercy from Christ our God.[10]

This is what an "ascended" humanity looks like: generous, solicitous of the poor, eager to reach out to the sick and suffering; it is vigilant for justice, concerned for righteousness, and deeply hospitable.

It looks like the Jesus who took shape in Mary's womb and grew and "went about doing good" (Acts 10:38 NKJV); the Jesus who keeps taking shape in human lives and going about doing good by the power of the Spirit to this very day.

That, by the way, is Luke's point in making the ascension the hinge of his two-volume work. If you've read the gospel of Luke and its sequel, the book of Acts, you may have noticed that one ends and the other begins with the ascension. There's a reason for that. Luke is telling us that Jesus' ascension to the Father (even though it entails a disappearance) does not *actually* take him out of the world but rather transforms and intensifies his presence within it—in the church. For the church's life in this world is nothing less than the ongoing life of the risen and ascended and now-reigning Christ.[11] As Paul writes: "And God placed all things under his feet and appointed him to be head over everything for the church, which is his body, the fullness of him who fills everything in every way" (Ephesians 1:22–23).

The church is not a social club that lives in the loving memory of its now-absent founder. It *is nothing less than the fullness of the Ascended One who now, by his church, fills everything in every way.*

EVERYTHING DONE WITHOUT US

I find all of this to be wildly relevant for the moment we are living in. We all—believer and unbeliever, saint and skeptic—worry about the fate of our common humanity, whether we are headed for the kingdom or for some world-ending calamity. The so-called myth of progress—the idea that humanity, all by itself, will keep improving—has suffered critical blows in the past hundred years, and cynicism is high in many quarters.

Some, however, are rather more bullish about our prospects. I'm not mad about that. In fact, I'm heartened—truly heartened—by the number of folks I run into who insist that we are not fated for disaster, that we have choices to make and a part to play in the elevation of our individual and common humanity. As hope is good for the soul, so it is good for the life of a society. And it is certainly preferable to the despair that ever crouches at our door.

Still, I wonder about it all—about whether this isn't just the latest attempt to save ourselves by our works, to climb to the heavens by building a bigger, better, sturdier tower. Didn't God scatter the people of Babel? Won't he do it again?

I listen to the podcasts on spirituality and self-improvement, like many of us do. I've gleaned a lot. But I wonder, and I worry. I worry about what it's all suggesting, whether it can really deliver what it promises—that if we just manage our diet and our exercise and our thought life and our sleep and learn to cultivate optimal brain wave patterns and get a couple side-hustles going and see a therapist regularly and add to it all a pinch of DIY spirituality, we'll achieve our utopia. We'll walk like gods upon the earth—just as we were meant to do.

But there's a hidden price tag. There always is. You're going to have to have space in your schedule to begin to build #yourbestlife. And money to join the gym and buy the right supplements (which, of course, the high priests of #yourbestlife are willing to sell you for the *very low price* of $99 per month).

And the right friends and support network to help you achieve all your dreams.

And while we're on the topic, you're going to have to cut out of your life everyone who might be an obstacle to your newfound vision of the good life—friends, family members, and even spouses who just don't get it. They can't be part of your life if they won't help you build the brand.

So, they tell us, eliminate them. In fact, ruthlessly eliminate from your life everyone who doesn't share your outlook or point of view. Yes, we know that this sounds brutal and difficult, but trust us, you have the right—an absolute right—to build your ideal community, to curate your ideal "family." Wholeness and happiness lie just on the other side of a little relational swashbuckling.

Trust us, it will be worth it.

When you get down to it, it all starts looking a little nefarious: a boutique yuppie religion of the upwardly mobile that benefits some and leaves out others. A secular spirituality of the socially privileged.

It's worth asking: Where does the single mother of three working two jobs to make ends meet fit here? Or the elderly retiree whose strength is diminishing and is confined to the nursing home? What about the migrant worker or the refugee? Or the developmentally disabled?

All of these and more are, I think, tragically left out, left behind. No room for them in the inn of self-salvation.

It seems to me that this is what we run into when the ascension of our humanity to the heavens is made an *achievement*. And that is precisely what the church *does not* say about the ascension of humanity.

We didn't do it. We never could. And we never will.

But God did it in Christ. "Everything for us has . . . already been done without us," says Kathryn Tanner.[12] It's all already "real" in him. As he ascended into the heavens, we ascended with him. We're there—slotted safely into the heavens of God's own life with the Ascended Christ, who "is our place within the life of the Trinity."[13] All we need to do is trust it, to receive it as a gift, by faith, together—and then watch what happens.

The gospel teaches us that humanity *will ascend* because in Christ, it *has already ascended*, and that no one is barred entry to that ascent who wishes to participate. As the church gathers week after week around the visibly invisible (invisibly visible?) presence of the Ascended One in sermon and song, in bread and cup, somehow, some way, it is transfigured. Humanity becomes all it was ever meant to be.

For there, in the gathered worship of the faithful, enemies are made friends. Estranged spouses are reconciled. Children's hearts are turned to their parents and parents' hearts to their children. The lonely are set in families. The vulnerable are protected and the young are celebrated and the aged are venerated. The marginalized are brought to the center and the poor are clothed with dignity and the disabled are honored and included as we all together fall down in worship as equals before the throne of God and of the Lamb, grateful for the redemptive work of God in Christ. As Richard John Neuhaus put it, Jesus brings

> the totality of all that love assumed; in the lead a thief who believed and half believed, followed by a ragtag band of tax collectors and sinners and the victims of history beyond numbering, victims who only now know the sacrifice of which their sacrifice was part. Choirs of angels, cherubim and seraphim come out to meet him, to welcome home the

Son of God. They stand aghast at the battered, tattered company he is bringing with him. "They are all mine," he says. "They are my brothers and sisters; they are the ones whom I went to seek and to save. I am taking them to the Father. I am taking them home."[14]

Chapter 7

QUESTIONS FOR DISCUSSION

1. Do you come from a church or tradition that taught about the ascension? If so, what is your understanding of it?

2. Is there a place in your life where knowing that Jesus is in charge might be a comfort to you?

3. "He took us with him to the heart of things." How did this chapter's discussion of ascension broaden your understanding of what it means to be "seated with Christ in the heavenly realms"?

PENTECOST

Transfiguring Life

He will baptize you with the Holy Spirit and fire.
—LUKE 3:16

As the Spirit shows his face, the church appears.
—ROBERT JENSON, *Systematic Theology*

No account of the sojourn of the Word in our midst can be considered complete without invoking Pentecost—the miracle recounted in Acts 2 in which the Spirit descends in power upon the early believers. The recently ascended Christ sends forth the Spirit, and with that, the church is born—which is, in a nutshell, the entire message of Acts.

I am grateful to have been raised in a religious milieu that welcomed and celebrated the work of the Spirit. Even more—that *sought encounters* with the Spirit. I have many memories of such encounters. They have all shaped me.

It's Wednesday night, around eight o'clock. The service has been underway for ninety minutes, and I am plastered to the floor, dead asleep, as the preacher waxes eloquent on the Mysteries.

Before long the congregation will rise again to sing and pray. And I will rise too, wiping the drool from my cheek and rubbing my face as in my stupor I try to reenter the whirl of the Spirit with them. Or maybe it is just possible that in my stupor I never really left it. "When I awake, I am still with you" (Psalm 139:18).

Whatever the case, I remember the warmth of those services—many of them conducted in the frigid heart of those long, dreadful Wisconsin winters. We'd gather out of the numbing cold and let the Spirit stoke the fires in our midst. Fires for God. For each other. Fires of love and joy. Fires that licked up the damp sadnesses that so often make life unlivable.

I remember people laughing and smiling.

A very great deal of my childhood happened in environments like that—environments where the saints gathered to seek the Face, to breathe the Breath. "Blow upon me, O Wind of God, breathe upon me, O Spirit of the Lord,"[1] we'd sing, and then open our hearts to receive whatever gifts the Spirit had to give. And the greatest gift, we believed, was quite simply the gift of the Spirit's own self. Nothing better than to have the Holy Spirit "fall" on you or "fill" you to overflowing.

It did something to you.

Changed you.

Our church had a school which I attended for many years. One day when I was in the fourth grade, a woman of God in her eighties named Ola came to teach our Bible class. She taught, if memory serves me, on the love of God that we can experience through the Holy Spirit. She used no notes. I remember *that* clearly. Just her open Bible and her long history with God, which she shared freely, effortlessly with us. I thought that was impressive.

When Ola was done teaching, she asked us if we would like to be filled with the Holy Spirit. We said yes, not knowing, really, what we were saying yes to; but we did it all the same. All of us did. And so Ola had us stand up from our desks and form a little circle in the middle of the classroom. And then she went around to each of us—a withered old woman in her eighties, no taller than the shortest of the ten-year-olds gathered there—and prayed that we might be filled with the Spirit.

I remember that her prayers—like her entire way of being—were exquisitely gentle. Without histrionics or bombast or fancy words, she'd either lay her hands—blue veins like so many rivers of life lying just underneath the gossamer skin of those agéd hands—or, alternatively, blow gently upon the foreheads of each of us saying, "Receive the Holy Spirit."

One after another, we hit the deck.

(I am sorely tempted to provide a defensive apologia for this phenomenon—what some have called "getting slain in the Spirit." But the better angels of my biblical memory restrain me. Across the canon of Scripture, when God shows up, people fall. And at the end of all things, *all* will fall. The Testimony is clear on this point.)

I lay on my back for the better part of an hour, maybe more. And if you ask me what I experienced during that hour, I will tell you all I know:

It was like waves of warm love washing over me.

I thought thoughts, to be sure. But the experience was not really a "thinking" experience. It was a "being" experience.

The experience of Love.

Which is the experience of God.

Which changes you.

"The Spirit of the LORD will come powerfully upon you," Samuel says to Saul, "and you will be changed into a different person" (1 Samuel 10:6).

What a promise.

When I finally got up off the floor, I remember walking more lightly. The world was brighter, less threatening. And I felt more secure in it.

I had other such encounters. During the summer between eighth and ninth grade, I was drowning in self-loathing. I'd lost my way the previous year and I knew it. Worse—it took being caught to get out. I felt not just guilty, but *ashamed*—ashamed that I'd abandoned what I knew was right, embarrassed that I wasn't able to help myself out of the mess. And though I'd repented and amended my ways, the self-loathing remained. I decided to take a week to fast and pray.

A week. At fourteen years old. Who even does that anymore?

Somewhere in the middle of the fast the Spirit met me. Exhausted and desperately hungry and fatigued from the heat of the day, I went into my room and closed the door and collapsed next to my bed and began to pour out my heart like water. Before long, words started to fail. The emotions were too deep, too powerful for any language I knew.

And I began to speak in tongues.

Not for the first time—or the last. Our church was charismatic, remember, which meant I'd been speaking in tongues since before I said the sinner's prayer or entered the waters of baptism (stick that one in your theological pipe and smoke it). But it *was* my first time praying in tongues *like this*: with genuine agony.

I prayed like my life depended on it. And as I did so—I don't know how else to describe this—the Spirit fell and began to yank the self-loathing out of my psyche by the roots.

I did not cry. I *wailed*. Heavy tears. Thick sobs. Heaves.

To this day I have no idea how long I was in that state. Three minutes? Thirty minutes? Three hours? I am not sure that it matters. Time, I have learned, does strange things in the divine hand. All I know is that when it was over, I was cleansed. The self-loathing never returned. Even to tell that story to you now is to evoke tears of gratitude.

WITH THE FATHER AND THE SON

I will say this as clearly as I can: *I love the Holy Spirit*, whom I have come to know more and more as the very Lord and Life-giver that the Nicene Creed proclaims him to be, the one who with the Father and the Son is *worshiped and glorified*.

I am a charismatic Christian, all the way down. My theological journey has led me back and forth across the expanse. From the early Apologists to the Greek Fathers to Augustine and Aquinas and the Reformers, right through to modern greats like Bonhoeffer and Barth and Wright. Likewise, my experiential journey of the faith has taken me from the Spirit-swirled gatherings of my charismatic upbringing to house churches and high churches and Bible churches and everything between. I've worshiped with Catholics and Baptists and Anglicans and Presbyterians and have been enriched by the variety of ways that every stream of Christianity bears witness to the life of holy devotion—from women of faith like Julian of Norwich and Teresa of Avila and Dorothy Day to men of God like Benedict of Nursia and Saint John of the Cross and Brother Lawrence.

But I will always be charismatic at heart.

My reasons, I have come to believe, are not a matter of mere preference. They are biblical.

"There is one coming more powerful than I," says John the Baptist to his hearers, "the straps of whose sandals I am not worthy to stoop down and untie. *He will baptize you with the Holy Spirit and with fire*" (Luke 3:16, paraphrased).

The Son baptizes with the Spirit. The Word gives the Breath. It is the capstone of Christ's redeeming work—the coming-to-term of his effort to save. After he is raised from the dead, he promises, "I am going to send you what my Father has promised; but stay in the city until you have been clothed with power from on high" (Luke 24:49). And he instructs, "Do not leave Jerusalem, but wait for the gift my Father promised, which you have heard me speak about. For John baptized with water, but in a few days, you will be baptized with the Holy Spirit" (Acts 1:4–5).

We have not fully encountered Jesus until we have been filled with the gift of his Spirit. There is no church, no people of God, apart from the Spirit. And therefore, our lives are not complete until we have said yes to all that the Spirit is and has.

THE LORD, THE GIVER OF LIFE

And yet we are reluctant.

So very reluctant.

I know this because I have felt the reluctance in my own soul. When I was in my early twenties, I began to question my charismatic upbringing. The abuses I saw in the movement appalled me. (They still do.) Sermons that had no mooring in the biblical text. Larger-than-life personalities that bore no resemblance to the Jesus of the Gospels. "Prophecies" that turned out to be little more than religious profiteering. And dubious political and cultural alliances.

So many dubious alliances . . .

I wanted nothing to do with it.

So I left. Went as far away from it as I could think of. To a Reformed seminary in the upper Midwest where I could hunker down, study the Bible and theology and church history, and get on with the serious business of church without having to deal with all the pseudo-pneumatic frivolity I'd grown so weary of.

For a year or so I set aside the Spirit. Gave my attention to other matters. Or tried to, anyway. But the Spirit has a way of seeking you out, setting the conditions for surprise. "Where can I go from your Spirit? Where can I flee from your presence?" (Psalm 139:7).

One day during my second year of seminary, I was reading a book of theology by an author whose name I have since forgotten. Reformed fella. And he was quoting another Reformed fella, whose name I *do* remember: the Dutch-American theologian Geerhardus Vos, who said this:

> The Spirit's proper sphere is the future aeon; from thence
> He projects Himself into the present, and becomes a prophecy of Himself in his eschatological operations.[2]

I know, I know. So abstruse as to be incomprehensible, right? But that's part of the humor of the story. I mean, of all the places to be ambushed by the Spirit—reading a crusty and obscure bit of Reformed theology. But honestly, I've come to see that's just like the Holy Spirit. There's a prodigality to his work. You never quite know where he's gonna show up—even (believe it or not) reading theology.

The line grabbed my attention. I sat with it for a while, and then suddenly I saw: if the work of God is to renew all things in Jesus Christ, the *power* of that renewing work is quite simply the Holy Spirit, who is the Life not only of God, but also of the age to come. And therefore when we come in contact with God the Holy Spirit, we are becoming participants even now in the "world without end" that the old songs and prayers of the church acclaim. The Spirit—and our lives entangled with the Spirit—becomes the Spirit's prophecy of the Spirit's own now-and-future life-giving operation.

Wild.

But there was a further consequence, which I also immediately saw: *apart from the Holy Spirit, access to the life of the age to come is not possible.*

For the Spirit *is* that life. The Nicene Creed says that the Spirit is the "the Lord, the Giver of Life." Which means that to reject the Spirit is to reject the one Life of God offered to us.

And, by the same token, to welcome the Spirit is to welcome Life—

Life healed.

Life elevated.

Life transfigured.

Life transformed.

The Spirit unites us with the Word made flesh, the Word Incarnate and crucified and now raised to life, the Word who gleefully hauls us up into the heavens with him. And so, just as the Spirit breathed upon his disciples, even now he breathes upon us and says: "Receive the Holy Spirit."

A PEOPLE OF THE GIFT

With that I saw I could reclaim my roots without any embarrassment—that to be a Christian at all is to be a person who has received the gift of the Spirit.

It is to be, in a word, *charismatic*—a person of the Gift; even if you don't claim the moniker "charismatic." And for the record, I don't think anyone *needs* to; my only dog in the fight is the conviction that the Spirit is what makes the church *the church.*

All the same, I am sometimes asked, for clarity's sake, what I mean when I use the term *charismatic*. I usually answer something like this:

> To be charismatic is to believe that God is not an idea
>   but the Living Heart of reality.
> It is to believe that God is right here, right now.
> Which means that anything can happen.

God the Spirit—ever-present among us—can break in and break out at any time, dazzling and renewing us with the life he is and has.

The stories I shared earlier in the chapter set the agenda, I think, for what it looks like when the life of the Spirit descends upon us:

> Loving, joyful community.
> Intimacy with God.
> Freedom and healing.

I believe this because I see it everywhere in the Scriptures, and because I have seen the pattern repeat itself before my very eyes for many years now. As a pastor, as a *Christian*, I never cease to be astonished by how the Spirit works, by what the Spirit does.

Two people who had been lifelong friends were feuding in a congregation I pastored years ago. The falling-out had been significant enough that it created ripples across our small community. Despite our best efforts, none of us who knew them seemed capable of bringing about a reconciliation. Total stalemate.

Holy Week rolled around. The two former friends attended at our Maundy Thursday service, where we gathered to remember the giving of Jesus' "new commandment" and the washing of his disciples' feet in John 13. I spoke of Jesus and the call to love one another and what the act of washing each other's feet symbolizes and enacts. We welcomed the Spirit and invited him to soften our hearts.

By some chance (and it was pure chance—I know this because I asked) the two wound up in the same line to get their feet washed. *And as luck would have it (or was it luck?), they were paired off to wash each other's feet.*

The Spirit fell like rain.

As they washed each other's feet, tears of repentance and forgiveness also fell. And the offense likewise fell—into the depths, never to return. And they were reconciled.

A work of the Spirit.

Another time I was leading a service of lament for a small group of people. I taught them about the power of lament. How God invites it. How the psalmists model it. And how when we lift our voices up to God in anger and frustration and protest, God draws near to us.

I then invited the group to enter a structured time of corporate and individual lament—expressing to God their pain and hurt and their questions about where he was when they suffered and what exactly he was doing to rectify it.

The corporate lament primed the pump. The individual lament let loose a flood. Some sobbed quietly. Others wailed. It was difficult to witness. And also, in its way, beautiful. Many were forging a rugged honesty with God for the very first time in their lives.

We took some time at the end of the service to debrief. I wanted to know: what was the experience like? What was God doing in you?

One young man said, "That was the most painful thing I've ever done," and then paused. I wondered—and worried—about what was coming next. Would I be denounced for pastoral malfeasance, for a profound act of ministerial irre-sponsibility? He continued: "And I've never felt so close to God in my entire life. Thank you."

A work of the Spirit.

Another time, a man came up to me after a service. "Can I talk to you?" he asked. He began to pour out one of the most painful tales I'd ever heard. Life had come together quickly for him in his early twenties. Fresh out of school, he promptly got married, started a business with his best friend, had a couple kids, and enjoyed a mostly unimpeded up-and-to-the-right existence for a decade or more.

Until his wife was diagnosed with cancer. Then his world began to come apart at the seams. She was his world.

His friend and business partner assured him, "Take all the time you need. I'll hold it down over here." So he did. His wife went through treatments for a couple of years, and he worked hard to parent their kids, who were also coming apart as their mom's life ebbed away.

She died of a brain tumor. He and his children buried her and grieved some, and then he went back to work, only to discover that while he was away, his friend had leveraged him out of the business.

The cumulative sense of loss and betrayal was simply too much to bear. He self-medicated, drinking and doping and buying stuff he didn't need. He and his kids eventually moved to another state to get away from the pain.

But pain doesn't work like that. It writes itself into your skin, your bones. Wherever you go, it goes; wherever you stay, it stays.

One day he was out with his new girlfriend and saw a "ser-vice times" banner hanging on the side of our building. He had never really been to church before but decided to give it a whirl. He came inside, grabbed a cup of coffee, sat down, sobbed through the whole service, and went home wondering what had happened to him.

He came back the next week.

And the next.

And the next.

And each time he returned the same thing would happen. He'd grab a cup, sit in the back, and sob.

"Pastor," he said, "I've been doing this week after week after week. I come here and bawl my eyes out. I'm feeling things that I've spent the last five years running away from. What is happening to me?"

He said this to me as I was standing next to one of my colleagues. The two of us looked at each other and smiled.

"*God* is happening to you, friend," we said. "You're grieving what needs to be grieved. You're being healed."

He took that in. Then asked, "What should I do?"

"Just trust it," we replied, "and keep showing up."

A work of the Spirit.

WHEN THE SPIRIT SHOWS HIS FACE

He did just that. Kept coming to the place where the saints are gathered and the Word is preached and the sacraments are administered; the place that Martin Luther called "The Gate of Heaven"[3]—the church.

And man, you oughta see this guy. His face shines—which is just what the Spirit does: bringing life to the scorched earth of our lives.

> Till the Spirit is poured on us from on high,
>> and the desert becomes a fertile field,
>> and the fertile field seems like a forest. (Isaiah 32:15)

And we are just those deserts. One church father, Basil the Great, said that whoever desires holiness or virtue in fact desires the Spirit since the Spirit is the source of both. "They are watered by his inspiration," Basil says, "and assisted toward their proper and natural end," which is God. God's Spirit lives, "but not because he has been restored to life; rather, he is the source of life itself." To drink of the Spirit is to drink Life like a desert drinks rain. Indeed, according to Basil, every good gift of God comes to us through the Spirit, including the greatest gift of all: "remaining in God, kinship with God, and the highest object of desire, becoming God."[4]

The Spirit, in a word, *deifies* us, taking us straight into the heart of God, where—to use a favorite image of the church fathers—our lives become incandescent with the light and heat of God's very self, like iron made red-hot *with* fire and *in* fire—which is, after all, the goal of the spiritual life: a union with God that penetrates to the very depths of our very being, overwhelming and overrunning every part of who we are; a union that endures in and even beyond our death, so that "when the fire of our own lives grows cold, we come to burn with God's own flame."[5]

Basil's reflections in *On the Holy Spirit* are striking not just for their rhetorical brilliance, but also for a theological maneuver that is too seldom appreciated or even made in our day. A few pages after his observations on the Spirit as the source of life, Basil writes, "Just as the Father is seen in the Son, so the Son is seen in the Spirit."[6]

So then, we might ask, *just where is the Spirit seen?* After all, Jesus himself compared the Spirit to the wind. We never see the wind directly; we only see its *effects* (John 3:8). So, what is the most obvious and visible *effect* of the Spirit?

Basil is unambiguous. The Spirit is seen in the existence of the worshiping community: "*In worship*," he writes, "the Holy Spirit is inseparable from the Father and the Son, for if you are outside of him, you will not worship at all."[7]

That there is a gathering of the saints whose lives together are being transformed is the sign that the Spirit of the Son who is the Image of the Father has been poured out, that the work of the Triune God in the world has come to full term—which is why the third stanza of the Nicene Creed runs straight from the Spirit to the visible church. Robert Jenson's remark is apt: "As the Spirit shows his face, *the church appears*."[8]

This is why—for all its flaws, and they are many—the church is so critical. It's the place on earth where the Presence is at its most dense. Where Jesus by his Spirit has promised to remain, to bind up evil and to loose the power of the kingdom:

> Truly I tell you, whatever you bind on earth will be bound in heaven, and whatever you loose on earth will be loosed in heaven. Again, truly I tell you that if two of you on earth agree about anything they ask for, it will be done for them by my Father in heaven. *For where two or three gather in my name, there am I with them.* (Matthew 18:18–20, emphasis added)

It is true, so very true: the Presence and power are too often smothered by our sin and foolishness, by error and strife. Still, they remain. The Light remains. And it may break out at any time. Our job—our *only* job—is to say yes to the presence of the lively, life-giving Spirit in our midst. And then to sit back to watch what happens.

NO BODY BUT YOURS

In an earlier chapter, I shared about the foster family at the church I now pastor. The foster parents are still doing their thing. Just as faithful as can be. And miracles keep happening around them.

About nine months ago, they received two little boys. Rescued from a chaotic household, they were in a chaos state when they arrived among us. Rambunctious, a bit scared, and skittish with adults. The foster parents asked us once again if we'd anoint the children with oil and pray that the Spirit might work the magic of the kingdom into their bones.

And, again, our response was enthusiastic and immediate.

I'm happy to tell you that gracious God has answered, mercifully answered, our prayers for those boys. Every week they walk in with their heads held higher, more secure, more ready to meet greeting with confident greeting.

"Lookin' good this morning, Big B!" I'll say to the older brother when the family walks in. He beams with pride and slaps me five as he marches through the double-doors and down the hall to his Sunday school classroom. It makes me smile.

So one morning we gather again in a classroom with Foster Mom and Foster Dad along with the boys and now, also, two new little girls. We learn some details about the girls' lives and prepare to pray. The boys—Big B in particular—are rambunctious as ever, but it's different now. They're responsive to us, present, engaged. Baby girl is in her foster mom's arms crying while her big sister turns pirouettes in her princess dress as she plays happily alongside Big B.

I pull a small vial of anointing oil out of my pocket and begin. We anoint the baby girl. We anoint her sister. And we pray fervent prayers over them.

When we're finished, I turn and ask for an update on the boys and their situation. The foster mom and dad give us a few more details, and then I kneel in front of Big B and ask if I can pray for him and his brother again. I honestly wonder what he'll say. The first time we did it, they (understandably) squirmed and writhed and seemed so very uncomfortable with our little ritual that was all so new to them.

This time, however, and much to my surprise, Big B shoots back a quick and confident affirmative. And as I kneel in front of him to pray, he looks me dead in the eye and says, "Could you pray that my mom and dad would make better decisions?"

My, oh my. The world we live in.

So I do just that. Smear oil on his and his brother's foreheads again and prayed the filling and preserving power of the Spirit upon them both, and also upon their mom and dad, that all the promises of God which are yes in Christ would be "amen'ed" in the flourishing of their family.

The Presence is thick in the room. We all sense it. That we are standing with Christ in a classroom made holy ground.

Now if that moment were the only such moment, it would have been a great morning. But it isn't. When I finish, Big B opens his eyes and says, "Can I pray for you?"

Says Jesus:

Whoever receives one of these little children in My name receives Me; and whoever receives Me, receives not Me but Him who sent Me. (Mark 9:37 NKJV)

Who am I to refuse God when he speaks?

I say yes. Then Big B does me one better. He gestures at the oil: "Can I have that?" he asks. I turn it over to him. And then Big B dips his finger in the vial and smears the sign of the cross on my forehead and the foreheads of his little bro and the two girls, along with his foster mom and dad and the rest of us gathered there, and he prays God's blessing over all of us.

Leaves me speechless. Just speechless.

A sovereign work of the Spirit.

All praise to the table-turning God.

Our life together, congregational life, set under the prevenient care of the Life-Giving Spirit, is a place of signs and wonders. A place where, among other things, the lonely are set in families, and kids from chaotic homes suddenly become priests of the Lord and ministers of our God. A place where the words attributed to Saint Teresa of Avila become true in surprising ways:

> Christ has no body but yours,
> No hands, no feet on earth but yours.
> Yours are the eyes with which he looks
> Compassion on this world.
> Yours are the feet with which he walks to do good.
> Yours are the hands, with which he blesses all the world.
> Yours are the hands.
> Yours are the feet.
> Yours are the eyes.
> You are his body.
> Christ has no body now on earth but yours.[9]

Which is what I love about it. Why—all its flaws and failures not withstanding, all *my* flaws and failures notwithstanding— I keep coming back.

And what is my role in all this, as this congregation's pastor-preacher?

A pretty modest one, I'd say:

Keep showing up.

Keep giving them the story of Jesus, told as a promise.

And keep watching for God, being alert for signs of his Presence.[10]

Because here and there—

sometimes on the platform,
sometimes in the pulpit,
sometimes in a hospital room,
and sometimes in a back classroom . . .
if we're paying attention . . .

We just may see the Spirit break through.

We just may catch a glimpse of that *strange and gracious light.*

Amen.

Chapter 8

QUESTIONS FOR DISCUSSION

1. What has been your experience with the Holy Spirit?

2. "When the Spirit shows his face, the church appears." In what ways has the church been an evidence of the Spirit to you? Where do you find such an idea to be difficult or challenging?

3. In what ways has this book deepened your appreciation for the ways of the Spirit in the church and the importance of congregational life?

ACKNOWLEDGMENTS

A book is always a community effort, and as such, there are many to recognize:

To the team at Herald Press—thank you for believing in this project. And particularly Sara Versluis—your careful eye and fine editorial work made this book better in every way. I can't tell you how much I appreciate you.

I couldn't be more grateful for my dear friend and literary agent Don Pape. "A friend is always loyal, and a brother is born to help in time of need" (Proverbs 17:17 NLT). You have been both: friend, brother, and one more—an advocate. Thank you. Much love and many blessings to you and Ruthie.

A special thanks to Winn Collier, Marilyn McEntyre, John Blase, and the entire Sacred Art of Writing doctoral cohort at Western Theological Seminary (class of '24), with whom and among whom these words were first nurtured. Our three years together were an experience of a lifetime. I learned so much from all of you. Thank you.

My undying gratitude to Pastor Brady Boyd and the entire New Life Church community, who opened their arms to us when we were in a very dark and lost and lonely place. You have become our "Antioch."

To New Life East—you have no idea how much you mean to me. I dedicated this book to you because it was through you that the Lord has restored to me so much of the joy of my pastoral calling. You've loved and honored and celebrated Mandi and me in more ways and at more times than I can count. I surely needed you more than you needed me and am so grateful for you.

And of course, to my bride Mandi of nearly a quarter-century and our four kids, Ethan, Gabe, Bella, and Liam—you are the endless delight of my life. I can't believe God has given us to each other.

NOTES

PRELUDE

1. R. S. Thomas, "The Chapel," in *R. S. Thomas Collected Poems, 1945–1990* (Orion, 2000), 276. Reproduced with permission of the Licensor through PLSclear.
2. "The watchful dragons of the heart" is a line from C. S. Lewis, "Sometimes Fairy Stories May Say What's Best to Be Said," in *On Stories: And Other Essays on Literature* (Harvest Books, 2002), 47. "Dazzling us gradually" is imagery from Emily Dickinson:

   > Tell all the truth but tell it slant—
   > Success in Circuit lies
   > Too bright for our infirm Delight
   > The Truth's superb surprise
   > As Lightning to the Children eased
   > With explanation kind
   > The Truth must dazzle gradually
   > Or every man be blind—

   Emily Dickinson, "Tell All the Truth but Tell It Slant—(1263)," https://www.poetryfoundation.org/poems/56824/tell-all-the-truth-but-tell-it-slant-1263.
3. "The story of Jesus told as a promise" is a summary of the major premise of Robert Jenson's *Story and Promise: A Brief Theology of the Gospel about Jesus* (Wipf and Stock, 2014).
4. St. Augustine quoted in Benjamin Quinn, *Christ, The Way: Augustine's Theology of Wisdom* (Lexham Press, 2022), 95.
5. Robert E. Webber, *Ancient-Future Time: Forming Christian Spirituality through the Christian Year* (Baker, 2004), 26.

CHAPTER 1

1. W. B. Yeats, "The Second Coming," available on Poets.org, last modified May 23, 2019, https://poets.org/poem/second-coming.
2. Gustavo Gutiérrez, *On Job: God-Talk and the Suffering of the Innocent* (Orbis, 1987), 8.
3. W. H. Auden, *For the Time Being: A Christmas Oratorio* (Princeton University Press, 2013), 7.

4. Gregory Orr, *Concerning the Book That Is the Body of the Beloved* (Copper Canyon Press, 2005), 98.

5. Karl Barth, *Church Dogmatics IV/1* (T&T Clark, 1961 Reprint), 725.

6. Jürgen Moltmann, *Theology of Hope* (Fortress Press, 1993), 85.

7. Karl Barth, *Church Dogmatics IV/3* (T&T Clark, 1962), 322.

8. Fleming Rutledge, *Advent: The Once and Future Coming of Jesus Christ* (Eerdmans, 2018), 13–14.

9. Moltmann, *Theology of Hope*, 85.

10. Robert W. Jenson, *Systematic Theology Volume 1: The Triune God* (Oxford University Press, 2001), 198. Emphasis in the original.

11. John Webster, *God Without Measure: Working Papers in Christian Theology, Volume 1: God and the Works of God* (T&T Clark, 2016), 132–33.

12. Bernard of Clairvaux, "Sermo 5, In Adventu Domini, 1–3" (Opera Omnia, Edit. Cisterc. 4, 1966), 188–90, Crossroads Initiative, originally posted November 30, 2021, https://www.crossroadsinitiative.com/media/articles/three-comings-of-the-lord-st-bernard/.

13. Pierre Teilhard de Chardin, "Patient Trust," in *Hearts on Fire: Praying with Jesuits*, ed. Michael Harter (Loyola Press, 2005), 102. Available online at https://www.ignatianspirituality.com/prayer-of-theilhard-de-chardin/.

14. Barth, *Church Dogmatics IV/1*, 725.

15. Bernard of Clairvaux, "Sermo 5, In Adventu Domini, 1–3."

16. Quoted in "Story of Our Patron," St. Catherine of Siena, accessed February 18, 2024, https://stcatherine-ml.org/story-of-our-patron.

CHAPTER 2

1. As quoted by Hans Urs Von Balthasar, *The Scandal of the Incarnation: Irenaeus Against the Heresies*, selected and introduced by Hans Urs Von Balthasar (Ignatius, 1990), 4.

2. Karl Barth, *Church Dogmatics IV/1* (T&T Clark, 1961 Reprint), 5.

3. C. S. Lewis, *Miracles* (HarperCollins, 2001), chap. 14.

4. William Blake, "America," in *William Blake: The Complete Poems* (Penguin Classics, 2004), 213.

5. Morten Lauridsen, "O Magnum Mysterium," Wikipedia, accessed February 18, 2024, https://en.wikipedia.org/wiki/O_magnum_mysterium_(Lauridsen).

6. Kathryn Tanner, *Jesus, Humanity, and the Trinity: A Brief Systematic Theology* (Fortress, 2001), 2.

7. I put "spiritual" in scare quotes because I don't think my childhood faith tradition actually prioritized the spiritual in the biblical sense at all. I think we prioritized the disembodied and mistook it for the spiritual.

8. Gustavo Gutiérrez, *We Drink From Our Own Wells: The Spiritual Journey of a People* (Orbis Books, 1985), 65.

9. Catherine Mowry LaCugna, *God for Us: The Trinity and Christian Life* (Harper Collins, 1993), 263. Emphasis in the original.

10. The Literature Network, "Fyodor Dostoevsky: The Brothers Karamazov, Chapter 41," Online Literature, accessed February 20, 2024, http://www.online-literature.com/dostoevsky/brothers_karamazov/41/.

11. Annie Dillard, *Holy the Firm* (Perennial, 1977), 72–73.

12. Mary Oliver, "To Begin With, the Sweet Grass," in *Devotions: The Selected Poems of Mary Oliver* (Penguin Classics, 2017), 78.

13. Henry David Thoreau, *Walden and Civil Disobedience* (Penguin Classics, 1986), 376.

14. John Webster, *The Domain of the Word* (T&T Clark, 2013).

15. St. Athanasius of Alexandria, *On the Incarnation* (Fig Publishing, 2013), 18.

16. C. S. Lewis, *The Weight of Glory and Other Addresses* (Collier, 1980), 18–19.

CHAPTER 3

1. St. Augustine, *The City of God: Book XXII* (Penguin Classics, 2003), chaps. 8 and 9, 1034. Emphasis added.

2. C. S. Lewis, *Miracles* (San Francisco: HarperCollins, 2001), 219–20.

3. Wendell Berry, *Sex, Economy, Freedom, and Community* (Pantheon, 1994), 103.

4. Robert Jenson, "Evil as Person" in *Theology as Revisionary Metaphysics: Essays on God and Creation*, ed. Stephen John Wright (Wipf and Stock, 2014), 137. Emphasis in the original.

5. Flannery O'Connor, *Mystery and Manners* (Farrar, Straus, and Giroux, 1970), 118.

6. Dorothy Sayers, *Letters to a Diminished Church* (W Publishing, 2004), 181.

7. Sayers, 182.

8. M. Scott Peck, *People of the Lie: The Hope for Healing Human Evil* (Simon and Schuster, 1998), 179.

9. Martin Luther King Jr., *Strength to Love* (1981), 53.

10. St. Athanasius of Alexandria, *On the Incarnation* (Fig Publishing, 2013), 70. Emphasis added.

CHAPTER 4

1. My friend Tommy Brown has a wonderful book-length treatment of the temptation narratives called *The Ache For Meaning: How the Temptations of Christ Reveal Who We Are and What We're Seeking* (NavPress, 2023). He argues that the temptations address three primary questions of the human heart: *Will I have enough? Am I enough? Do I matter?*

2. Fyodor Dostoevsky, *The Brothers Karamazov*, trans. Constance Garnett (Barnes and Noble Classics, 2004), 236.

3. Chris Green, "Discerning Christ in the Old Testament, Part 2," *Essential Church Podcast*, 20:20, October 6, 2022, https://theessential.church/episode-137-discerning-christ-in-the-old-testament-with-chris-green-part-2/. In fact, Green says that the judgments of the Old Testament are almost always followed by something worse. The straight-on divine power embodied in the judgments, in other words, tends to make things *worse* not better.

4. Eugene Peterson, *Five Smooth Stones for Pastoral Work* (Eerdmans, 1980), 152.

5. Marilynne Robinson, *Gilead* (Farrar, Straus, and Giroux, 2004), 129.

6. Robert Farrar Capon, *Kingdom, Grace, Judgment: Paradox, Outrage and Vindication in the Parables of Jesus* (Eerdmans, 2002), 16. This book is indispensable reading for understanding how the parables fit within the entire strategy of Jesus. You won't always agree. But you won't see Jesus the same way, either.

7. Capon, *Kingdom, Grace, Judgment*, 16.

8. Capon, 17.

9. Marilynne Robinson, *Reading Genesis* (Farrar, Straus, and Giroux, 2024), 213.

10. Robinson, *Reading Genesis*, 217.

11. Capon, *Kingdom, Grace, Judgment*, 17.

12. Capon, 18–19.

13. Capon, 19.

14. John Paul II, "Redemptoris Missio: On the Permanent Validity of the Church's Missionary Mandate," Vatican, December 7, 1990, https://www.vatican.va/content/john-paul-ii/en/encyclicals/documents/hf_jp-ii_enc_07121990_redemptoris-missio.html. Italics in the original.

15. A little theological coda here. When I say "can't," it's not because God is constrained by something outside of himself. It's because he set the rules of relationship—and intends to respect them, whatever the costs. And indeed he has already borne the cost—for the cross is the cost to God for God to be God the way he has chosen to be God: God with us, God for us, forever, in a non-coercive, utterly free relationship of love.

16. Catherine Mowry LaCugna, *God for Us: The Trinity and Christian Life* (Harper One, 1993), 258.

17. C. S. Lewis, *The Screwtape Letters* (Bantam Books, 1982), 23.

18. Dostoyevsky, *The Brothers Karamazov*, 230.

19. Kathryn Tanner, *Jesus, Humanity, and the Trinity: A Brief Systematic Theology* (Fortress, 2001), 62.

20. Kristin Kobes Du Mez, *Jesus and John Wayne: How White Evangelicals Corrupted a Faith and Fractured a Nation* (Liveright, 2020), 3.

21. Katelyn Beaty, *Celebrities for Jesus: How Personas, Platforms, and Profits Are Hurting the Church* (Brazos Press, 2022).

22. Dostoyevsky, *The Brothers Karamazov*, 241. Emphasis added.

23. Henri Nouwen, *In the Name of Jesus* (Crossroad, 1989), 76–77.

24. St. Irenaeus of Lyons in *The Scandal of the Incarnation: Irenaeus Against the Heresies*, selected and introduced by Hans Urs Von Balthasar, trans. John Saward (Ignatius, 1990), 15.

25. Ronald Rolheiser, *The Holy Longing: The Search for a Christian Spirituality* (Image, 2019), 187.

CHAPTER 5

1. Portions of this chapter first appeared in Andrew Arndt, "Embracing Lent: The Art of Dying Well," Missio Alliance, February 21, 2023, https://www.missioalliance.org/embracing-lent-the-art-of-dying-well/.

2. Richard John Neuhaus, *Death on a Friday Afternoon* (Basic Books, 2000), xi–xii.

3. Dietrich Bonhoeffer, *Letters and Papers from Prison* (Touchstone, 1997), 361.

4. C. S. Lewis, *Out of the Silent Planet* (Scribner, 1996), 140.

5. Benedicta Ward, *The Sayings of the Desert Fathers: The Alphabetical Collection* (Cistercian Publications, 1984), 230.

6. John O'Donohue, "For Death," in *To Bless the Space Between Us* (Convergent, 2008), 72.

7. Jürgen Moltmann, *The Crucified God* (Fortress Press, 1993), 4.

8. Elie Wiesel, *Night* (Hill and Wang, 2006), 64–65.

9. Wiesel, *Night*, 68.

10. James Cone, *The Cross and the Lynching Tree* (Orbis, 2011), 21, 26.

11. Julian of Norwich, *Showings* (Paulist, 1978), 143.

12. John Calvin, *Institutes of the Christian Religion*, trans. Henry Beveridge (Peabody, MA: Hendrickson Publishers, 2008), Book 2, 330.

13. Calvin, *Institutes*, 332.

14. G. K. Chesterton, *Orthodoxy* (Image Books, 2001), 145. If Chesterton is right (and I think he is), it's arguable that one can't even really be an atheist anymore, for God is there too, crying out in the hell of the worst kind of spiritual and existential doubt, harrowing it by filling it with his presence. "Where can I go from your Spirit? Where can I flee from your presence?" (Psalm 139:7).

15. "A bright abyss" is a phrase borrowed from Christian Wiman's brilliant meditation on suffering, *My Bright Abyss* (Farrar, Straus, and Giroux, 2013).

16. T. F. Torrance, *The Mediation of Christ* (Helmers and Howard, 1992), 43.

17. I am not arguing for a universalist position—the idea that all will be saved. I'm with the folks who hold that part of the cost of our freedom is that we may finally reject God. What I'm arguing for here is that *even if we reject God*, we can only do so "within" God, as it were—since by the work of Jesus, even separation from God has been taken into God. "The descent of Christ into hell," Fleming Rutledge explains, "means that there is no realm anywhere"—not the realm of doubt, nor despair, nor deconstruction—"where anyone can go to be cut off from the saving power of God." *The Crucifixion: Understanding the Death of Jesus Christ* (Eerdmans, 2015), 463. Or as C. S. Lewis put it: "The doors of hell are locked from the inside." *The Problem of Pain* (Harper, 1996), 130.

18. Episcopal Church, *The Book of Common Prayer* (Oxford University Press, 1979), 281.

19. "There is no pit so deep that He is not deeper still" is sometimes attributed to Corrie Ten Boom but was in fact spoken by her sister Betsie not long before her death at the Ravensbrück concentration camp during the Holocaust. Remarkably, during her final days, Betsie began to dream of a house much larger than the one in which the Ten Boom family had hidden Jews—a house to rehabilitate not only those who had survived the horrors of the concentration camps, *but also* those Germans whose souls had been wounded by the atrocities they committed—a dream made possible by the gospel of God's reconciling love. Said Betsie to Corrie, over and over again, "We must tell people what we have learned here. We must tell them that there is no pit so deep that He is not deeper still." From *The Hiding Place* by Corrie Ten Boom with John and Elizabeth Sherrill (Bantam, 1971), 217.

20. Phillip Cary, *Jonah: Brazos Theological Commentary on the Bible* (Baker, 2008), 76.

21. Gustavo Gutiérrez, *On Job: God-Talk and the Suffering of the Innocent* (Orbis, 1987), 9.

CHAPTER 6

1. "President Clinton at a Dinner Honoring Rep. John Lewis (2000)," April 14, 2000, video, 1:27:30, https://www.youtube.com/watch?v=sNma1Dlp5TU.

2. Krista Tippett, "John Lewis: Love in Action," Onbeing, last updated July 23, 2020, https://onbeing.org/programs/john-lewis-love-in-action/.

3. Robert Jenson, *Can These Bones Live?* (Oxford University Press, 2016), 32–33.

4. Quoted in Vista Editorial Team, "Optimism or Despair?," Lausanne Europe, January 23, 2020, https://www.lausanneeurope.org/optimism-or-despair/.

5. Viktor Frankl, *Man's Search for Meaning* (Beacon Press, 2006), 74.

6. Frankl, *Man's Search for Meaning*, 75.

7. Bill and Gloria Gaither, "Because He Lives," Gaither Recording Studio, first recorded in 1971.

8. Jürgen Moltmann, *Theology of Hope* (Fortress Press, 1993), 21. Emphasis added. Emphasis added.

9. Susannah Heschel, Introduction to *Thunder in the Soul: To Be Known by God* by Abraham Joshua Heschel (Plough Publishing House, 2021), xxii.

10. Wendell Berry, "Manifesto: The Mad Farmer Liberation Front," in *The Selected Poems of Wendell Berry* (Counterpoint Press, 1999), 88.

11. Eugene Peterson, *Five Smooth Stones for Pastoral Work* (Eerdmans, 1980), 159.

12. Gustavo Gutiérrez, *We Drink From Our Own Wells*, (Orbis Books, 1985), 118.

13. United States Conference of Catholic Bishops, "Prophets of a Future Not Our Own," USCCB, accessed February 24, 2024, https://www.usccb.org/prayer-and-worship/prayers-and-devotions/prayers/prophets-of-a-future-not-our-own.

14. Robert W. Jenson, *Systematic Theology Volume 1: The Triune God* (Oxford University Press, 2001), 44.

CHAPTER 7

1. John Calvin, *Institutes of the Christian Religion*, trans. Henry Beveridge (Hendrickson Publishers, 2008), 335. Emphasis added.

2. Robert Farrar Capon, *Kingdom, Grace, Judgment: Paradox, Outrage and Vindication in the Parables of Jesus* (Eerdmans, 2002), 17–18.

3. Julian of Norwich, *Showings* (Paulist Press, 1978), 225. Italics mine.

4. Malcom Guite, *Sounding the Seasons: Seventy Sonnets for the Christian Year* (Canterbury Press Norwich, 2012), 45. Emphasis added.

5. Karl Barth, *Church Dogmatics IV/2* (T&T Clark, 1958), 21. Emphasis added.

6. Calvin, *Institutes*, 336. Emphasis added.

7. Julie Canlis, *Calvin's Ladder: A Spiritual Theology of Ascent and Ascension* (Eerdmans, 2010), 2. Emphasis added.

8. Catherine Mowry LaCugna, *God for Us: The Trinity and Christian Life* (Harper Collins, 1993), 263. Emphasis in the original.

9. Khaled Anatolios, *Deification through the Cross* (Eerdmans, 2020), 381.

10. Anatolios, *Deification through the Cross*, 388.

11. This is why so much of what happens in Acts parallels what happens in Luke. Read them with that in mind sometime. It's eye-opening.

12. Kathryn Tanner, *Christ the Key* (Cambridge University Press, 2010), 101.

13. Tanner, *Christ the Key*, 141.

14. Richard John Neuhaus, *Death on a Friday Afternoon* (Basic Books, 2000), 239.

CHAPTER 8

1. Joannah Glaeser, "Blow Upon Me, O Wind of God," Living Word Bible College, Adm. by ZionSong Music, 1983.

2. Geerhardus Vos, *The Pauline Eschatology* (P&R Publishing, 1994), 165.

3. Robert Jenson, *The Triune Story: Collected Essays on Scripture*, ed. Brad East (Oxford University Press, 2019), 266.

4. St. Basil the Great, *On the Holy Spirit* (St. Vladimir's Seminary Press, 2011), 53–54.

5. Kathryn Tanner, *Jesus, Humanity, and the Trinity: A Brief Systematic Theology* (Fortress, 2001), 110. The notion of "becoming God" was a common one among the fathers and mothers of the early church. "Deification" is what they normally called it—and by it they meant not that there was (or could be) any confusion between God and us. God is God and humans are humans—and each remains so, without confusion, forever. But because of the union God has achieved for us in the God-Man, Jesus Christ, by surrendering fully to the Spirit, human beings could be so taken into God that the line between where God ends and we begin could be so blurred as to be practically invisible, or at least irrelevant. Consider, for example, Jesus' teaching on the vine and the branches in John 15. Where does the vine end and the branch begin? . . . Exactly.

6. St. Basil the Great, *On the Holy Spirit*, 103.

7. St. Basil the Great, 103. Emphasis added.

8. Robert W. Jenson, *Systematic Theology Volume 1: The Triune God* (Oxford University Press, 2001), 89. Emphasis added.

9. Saint Teresa of Avila, "Christ Has No Body but Yours," Catholic Link, accessed February 24, 2024, https://catholic-link.org/quotes/st-teresa-of-avila-quote-christ-has-no-body-but-yours/.

10. "Be alert for signs of his presence" appears in Psalm 105:4 (*The Message*).

THE AUTHOR

Andrew Arndt is the lead pastor of New Life East, one of seven congregations of New Life Church in Colorado Springs, where he also hosts the *Essential Church* podcast, a weekly conversation designed to strengthen the thinking of church and ministry leaders. He previously served as lead pastor of Bloom Church, a neo-monastic, charismatic, liturgical, justice-driven network of house churches in Denver. He holds a DMin in the sacred art of writing from Western Theological Seminary (2024) and an MDiv from Trinity Evangelical Divinity School (2006). He has written for Missio Alliance, Patheos, *The Other Journal*, and *Mere Orthodoxy*. He is the author of *Streams in the Wasteland* and *All Flame*. He and Mandi have been married since 2000, and are grateful parents to four kids: Ethan, Gabe, Bella, and Liam.